For Marion

The Will and the Word

The Poetry of Edward Taylor

William J. Scheick

University of Georgia Press

Library of Congress Catalog Card Number:
71–190049
International Standard Book Number:
0–8203–0314–3

The University of Georgia Press, Athens 30602

ᴄ ᴄ

Acknowledgments

Grateful acknowledgment is made to the editors of the following journals who have published portions of this book and who have graciously granted permission to reprint copyrighted material:

Early American Literature. For "A Viper's Nest, the Featherbed of Faith: Edward Taylor on the Will," 5 (Fall 1970), 45–56. Copyright 1970 by the Early American Literature Group of the Modern Language Association.

Language and Style. For "Tending the Lord in All Admiring Style: Edward Taylor's *Preparatory Meditations*," 4 (Summer 1971), 163–87. Copyright 1971 by the Board of Trustees of Southern Illinois University.

Tennessee Studies in Literature. For "Man's Wildred State and the Curious Needlework of Providence: The Self in Edward Taylor's *Preparatory Meditations*," 17 (1972), 129–37. Copyright 1972 by the University of Tennessee Press.

Texas Studies in Literature and Language. For "Nonsense from a Lisping Child: Edward Taylor on the Word as Piety," 13 (Spring 1971), 39–53. Copyright 1971 by the University of Texas Press.

Contents

Part Three: Poet

Introduction

Although they apparently never published a treatise on the subject, New England Puritan thinkers, from the earliest to Jonathan Edwards, were so familiar with the Renaissance idea of the soul's faculties that it represented a virtually unquestioned premise for their numerous writings. Taught, as a subsection of physics, throughout the seventeenth century at Harvard,[1] this legacy from Aristotle and the Scholastics became firmly entrenched in the Puritan mind, where it long remained resistant to newer ideas fomenting in Europe.

The Puritans' acceptance of this concept was reinforced by their esteem for the writings of Augustine. Augustine, Perry Miller has noted, "exerted the greatest single influence upon Puritan thought next to that of the Bible itself"; in their writings one encounters "the turn of mind and sense of values, even sometimes the very accent of Augustine."[2] To a

1. Samuel E. Morison, *Harvard College in the Seventeenth Century*, 1: 247; Perry Miller, *The New England Mind*, 2:134.

2. Miller, *New England Mind*, 1:4, 5.

significant extent, then, the central body of Christian learning represented by the writings of this church father provided a foundation for much of Puritan thought. The Puritans were not familiar with his work only secondhand; for despite a general rule not to cite sources, references to him frequently occur in their sermons. In fact direct quotations from his writings are cited in such disparate books as Nathaniel Ward's *The Simple Cobler of Aggawam in America* (1647) and Increase Mather's *The Life and Death of That Reverend Man of God, Mr. Richard Mather* (1670). Even as late and sophisticated a Puritan as Jonathan Edwards, recent studies tell us, relied to a significant extent upon the thought of Augustine.[3] One might also bear in mind the suggestion that the Harvard curriculum of the time was founded on Augustine's *De Doctrina Christiana*.[4]

Edward Taylor (1642?–1729), an orthodox Puritan who lived and studied in England until 1668 and who attended Harvard after his arrival in America, inherited this theory of the soul's faculties. Of particular significance to him, as poet as well as minister, was the behavior of the will in this system; for, as the first part of this book will argue, the will symbolizes the whole man, serves as the seat of either sin or grace, and possesses the power to verbalize. As the last two sections of this study will indicate, it was particularly the relation between the will and its words which became the main focus of Taylor's poetic meditations.

In the following discussion I will also contend that Taylor held a high regard for Augustine, whose works provided a traditional frame of reference for the poet's view of the facul-

3. See the introductory comments to Jonathan Edwards, *A Treatise Concerning Religious Affections*, ed. John E. Smith, pp. 25, 45 (hereafter cited as *Religious Affections*); Douglas J. Elwood, *The Philosophical Theology of Jonathan Edwards*, pp. 77, 153; and Peter Gay, *A Loss of Mastery: Puritan Historians in Colonial America*, pp. 91, 94.

4. Arthur C. Norton, "Harvard Text-books and Reference Books of the Seventeenth Century," *Publications of the Colonial Society of Massachusetts*, 28 (April 1933), 361; see also pp. 367–69.

ties of the soul. Not only did he own at least part of an edition of Augustine's complete works,[5] but often this respect for the "clearer man" who lived in "clearer times" (TCLS, p. 15)[6] is overtly declared in his sermons, in which Augustine and Origen are the two church fathers most frequently cited.[7] Throughout Taylor's poetry one finds Augustinian doctrine implicit. Indeed we might readily draw certain analogies between the nature of Taylor's *Preparatory Meditations* and that of

5. It is at present impossible to say precisely how many of Augustine's works Taylor knew or owned. Thomas H. Johnson has reported that *Omnium operum* (Paris, 1531–32) was the set—whether whole or in part is not noted—the poet owned (*The Poetical Works of Edward Taylor*, 1939; reprint ed., Princeton: Princeton University Press, 1966, p. 204, no. 5). Donald E. Stanford, questioning the accuracy of Johnson's interpretation of the inventory of Taylor's library, suggests that the poet may have possessed only one volume of the set ("Two Notes on Edward Taylor," *Early American Literature*, 6, Spring 1971, 89). Thomas and Virginia Davis, offering *Omnium operum* (Basil, 1529) as the text, argue for several volumes ("Edward Taylor's Library: Another Note," *Early American Literature*, 6, Winter 1972, 271–73). The actual entry reads, "Austini Tomus Nonus operum fol: 18s," and may in fact refer to one of the several editions of Augustine merely entitled *Operum*, of which a few are actually in nine tomes (one may finally have to differentiate between tome or fascicle and volume in solving this problem). Taylor's quotations from Augustine do not help; they are, to be sure, drawn from a large number of the church father's works, but sometimes a passage is actually drawn from another text—Joseph Mead's *Works*, for example (Johnson, *Poetical Works of Edward Taylor*, p. 220, no. 192). What we do know is that Taylor owned some of Augustine's writings, that he collected Augustinian passages from the works of others, and that he reflects Augustine's thought, explicitly and implicitly, in his own work. This is ample warrant, I think, for considering the Augustinian influence on Taylor's beliefs. See also Robert N. Boll and Thomas M. Davis, "Saint Augustine and Edward Taylor's Meditation 138 (2)," *English Language Notes*, 8 (March 1971), 183–85.

6. For the sake of convenience Taylor's prose is cited by page reference in the text and is identified by c for *Edward Taylor's Christographia*, ed. Norman S. Grabo and TCLS for *Edward Taylor's Treatise Concerning the Lord's Supper*, ed. Norman S. Grabo. Quotations from his poetry are from *The Poems of Edward Taylor*, ed. Donald E. Stanford. Each poem of the *Preparatory Meditations* is referred to by number (1.17, 10, for instance, designates the tenth line of the seventeenth poem in the first series); those of *Gods Determinations* will be signified by GD and the appropriate page number.

7. It is interesting to note, for example, that in regard to the question of how Original Sin is transmitted, Taylor argued not for the more common New England view of imputation but for Augustine's concept of its propagation through "the Spermatick Principalls" (c, pp. 13–14). Thomas Werge suggests that Augustine may also be the source of Taylor's tree-of-life imagery: "The Tree of Life in Edward Taylor's Poetry: The Sources of a Puritan Image," *Early American Literature*, 3 (Winter 1969), 200.

Augustine's *Confessions*, not the least of which would be their mutual introspective inquiry conducted in a meditative spirit and focused on the nature of conversion.

It would be mistaken, however, to conclude that Augustinian influence on Taylor's thought displaced his Calvinist heritage. Indeed in many respects Calvin was responsible for Puritan sensitivity to Augustine. Moreover, Taylor's teachings always remained consistent with the five points of the Synod of Dort (1618–19): total depravity, unmerited election, limited atonement, irresistible grace, and the perseverance of the saints. But Taylor and other Puritan divines often turned to earlier church fathers, particularly regarding matters not fully treated by Calvin. One such question concerned conversion, specifically how one is to prepare for it and what stages are experienced by the saint. Calvin was less interested in the process of conversion than in its fact. So it is not surprising to detect direct Augustinian influence in Taylor's work. My discussion, then, assumes certain similarities of thought between the two men and refers to Augustine's writings in order to elucidate matters suggested or implied in the Puritan poet's verse. This procedure may at times give the impression that Taylor was exclusively Augustinian, but I hope the reader will bear in mind the limits within which such comparisons are actually being made.

It is fair to say that Taylor's fascination with the theory of faculty psychology and theological tenets rarely became enmeshed in technical jargon. Although he was often concerned with those intricacies and fine distinctions which seem to have preoccupied countless other Puritan divines, analytical debates over abstruse issues in regard to the faculties rarely crept into his sermons. Taylor saw the value of the sermon as lying in its personal relevance or meaning to his parishioners as well as to himself whose duty it was to serve as an ambassador of Christ. Abstract or moot arguments might represent an impediment to the task of winning souls. Consequently he addressed his psychological and theological concerns primarily to one consideration: the nature of conversion. He recognized that the determination of one's spiritual state was the single most difficult enigma each sincere Puritan had to confront. This solitary encounter with the inner self was, in fact, so pivotal in Puritan lives that it ultimately nurtured such heretical beliefs—embedded in the very origins of Puritanism—as Arminianism and antinomianism.[8]

Although the subject matter of Taylor's extant sermons chiefly pertains to Christ and the Lord's Supper, there is evident throughout them a distinct concern with the experience of conversion. *Gods Determinations*, Taylor's long poem depicting the various trials of the elect in the temporal word, is almost entirely devoted to this question. But both his sermons and this poem were designed for an audience, whereas the *Preparatory Meditations*, in which I am primarily interested in this study, was private. These poems of personal devotion narrate Taylor's own search for conversion. Like Augustine, Taylor learned to look within himself in search for truth and divine favor; and like the *Confessions*, the *Preparatory Meditations* reflects a heartfelt response to this inward experience. It is not surprising, therefore, that similar to the *Confessions*, Taylor's meditations fail to provide a systematic theology but rather offer an individual, if traditionally oriented, synthesis of a very personal faith.

Taylor noted in his "Spiritual Relation" that he had undergone a spiritual awakening at an early age and that the elect are truly able to arrive at some degree of assurance,[9] but he never permitted himself the dangerous and possibly damning luxury of comfortably identifying with God's chosen. An assured hope in his election was permissible, a hope motivating an introspective search for clues to God's favor. As the *Preparatory Meditations* clearly indicates, Taylor shaped his psychological notions and christological thought into an intense inquiry into the state of his soul. The outcome of this endeavor would, in Taylor's view, always remain unresolved in this world; for the regenerative process, which inspires this search, is terminated only in heaven. For Taylor, the words of his poetic meditations, derived from and incorporating the vicissitudes of daily life, dramatize this quest. Since they are conceived in the will, the central faculty of the

8. Alan Simpson presents this aspect of the Puritans in *Puritanism in Old and New England*.

9. Donald E. Stanford, "Edward Taylor's 'Spiritual Relation,'" *American Literature*, 35 (January 1964), 467–75.

soul, words become events which mirror one's spiritual disposition. Thus the *Preparatory Meditations* was for its author an expression of his self, a self seeking in an experiential context for a true identity based on the love of Christ. Indeed, the poet's search for conversion is a quest for love—both Christ's and his own in response to that of Christ—and this is the central theme of the *Preparatory Meditations*, as it is of the writings of Augustine. To concentrate on this theme of love is, I think, to perceive the underpinning of the *Preparatory Meditations*. For Taylor, in typical Puritan fashion, divine love is paradoxically both the lowest common denominator and the epitome of all creation. God's love is, in Taylor's view, synonymous with being, or life; it is the *Aqua Vitae* or grace that imbues and animates everything.

In order to arrive at an understanding of his poetic self and its verbal quest for divine love or conversion, the discussion of the first three chapters begins this study with a survey of Taylor's conception of reason, nature, the human body, and the will. A consideration of these subjects—especially the nature of the will, its role in loving, and its relation to language—unearths several ideas which inform, consciously and unconsciously, the poet's questing self and which necessarily are embedded in the substrata of his verse. To some extent these chapters run the risk of appearing to argue for a monolithic view of the ideas under discussion. In order to clarify or amplify Taylor's beliefs, for instance, reference is made to the writings of such diverse Puritan authors as Thomas Hooker, John Cotton, James Fitch, Increase Mather, Benjamin Wadsworth, Samuel Willard, and even Jonathan Edwards.[10] Perhaps the insight derived from such a proce-

---

10. Such reference to Edwards is valid, I think, because contrary to Perry Miller's portrait of him as forward looking (*Jonathan Edwards*), Edwards was, as Peter Gay somewhat offhandedly describes him in *A Loss of Mastery*, "the last medieval American—at least among the intellectuals" (p. 116). And Edward Davidson notes: "In his own time Edwards was an anomaly. He seemed to his contemporaries to be the passionate supporter of a body of doctrine and thought which, if not discredited altogether, was at best inappropriate to the times and to the lives men lead in this world" (*Jonathan Edwards: The Narrative of a Puritan Mind*, p. 146). From this perspective it seems to me quite proper to cite Edwards, albeit with much discretion, in certain instances to clarify facets of Taylor's beliefs.

dure inescapably endorses Perry Miller's sense that beneath individual differences there indeed do exist points of tangency in regard to fundamental aspects of Puritan thought; these elements of coherence, it must be admitted, were doubtless reinforced by Puritan respect for Augustine's writings as well as by their more general inheritance of Augustinian tradition. My debt to Miller notwithstanding, I recognize that the trend of recent studies of Puritanism properly argues for a pluralistic reading of the culture. In this light I have cited other divines with caution, seeking primarily only to illuminate Taylor's views.

In chapter 4 the ideas considered in the preceding discussions are related to Taylor's christological thought in order to explain further his emphasis on verbal piety. Chapter 5 considers the poet's artistry. It is, in a sense, the climax of this study, for it attempts to suggest how, in the light of his private search for conversion, Taylor's interpretation and adaption of his psychological and theological beliefs led him to write the sort of poetry found in the *Preparatory Meditations*. This chapter investigates what I take to be Taylor's conscious idea of poetic decorum, particularly as manifested in his style and use of metaphor. The final chapter considers the poet's alleged mysticism and emphasizes the poetic self's quest for love and identity. What will emerge from the "blot and blur" of my discourse—"It would appear as dawbing pearls with mud"—will be, I hope, an integrated portrait of why and how Taylor discerned the drama of his conversion to lie in the personal experience of humbly and fully devoting himself, as poet and as minister, to the praise and service of the Word. Especially significant is how this praise and service was manifested in Taylor's pious, loving words.

Concerning the outcome of this study the author has only himself to blame and many to thank. I am especially indebted to many scholars and friends:

To Edward H. Davidson, who enthusiastically encouraged my pursuit of this study and who provided thoughtful guidance during its earlier stages.

To Frank Hodgins and Ernest N. Kaulbach for their helpful advice; and to Arthur E. Barker, whose influence on my approach to Taylor is boldly undisguised.

To Jerome Mitchell, of the University of Georgia, and Alan Day, researcher of the British Museum, who both made possible a collation and photocopy of the title page and index of the 1531–32 edition of Augustine's works.

To Ms. Frances B. McMahon, curator of the Edwin Smith Historical Museum of the Westfield Athenaeum, for her more than gracious assistance with the Westfield "Church Record"; and to Donald T. Gibbs, librarian of the Redwood Library and Athenaeum, for his help with several Taylor manuscripts.

To Donald E. Stanford and Norman S. Grabo for making so much of Taylor's writings available and for the firm foundation they have provided for future students of Taylor's work.

To the English Department and the Graduate College of the University of Illinois at Urbana as well as to the University of Texas Research Institute for financial assistance at various stages of this book.

To my colleagues in the Department of English at the University of Texas at Austin for an invigorating sense of community, especially to David DeLaura.

And, of course, to Marion, my wife, who lent her faith and energy to bringing this book to completion and from whom I accepted patient assistance without sufficient thanks.

Part One: Will

Chapter I

Like Children's Catching
Speckled Butterflies

Reason and Nature

Although they derived much of their theology from Calvin's teachings, New England Puritans readily called into question, as early as the seventeenth century, many of the specific tenets set forth in his writings.[1] Their renewed religious vigor, their sense of special calling, and their intellectual inheritance contributed to the Puritan need to elucidate or modify aspects of Calvin's thought. Two of the areas in which certain Puritan divines differed from his views concern the role of human reason in conversion and the place of physical nature in the divine scheme.

Fallen man, according to Calvin, forfeited for the most part whatever powers his rational faculty may have originally pos-

1. See, for instance, Samuel E. Morison, *Builders of the Bay Colony*, p. 57; and Everett H. Emerson, "Calvin and Covenant Theology," *Church History*, 25 (June 1956), 136–44. Thomas M. Davis notes that "Taylor's demonstrable knowledge of Calvin's *Institutes* and the condemnations which Calvin makes of Origen's methods and interpretations could hardly have gone unnoticed by Taylor, yet he is apparently unmoved by Calvin's judgment" ("Edward Taylor and the Traditions of Puritan Typology," *Early American Literature*, 4, 1970, 32).

sessed, with the consequence that he has become totally helpless and dependent upon God's arbitrary mercy or wrath. Partly informing this notion of man's complete vulnerability was Calvin's effort to repudiate the Christian-humanist regard for reason, a regard which allowed for the prominence of this faculty in the experience of conversion.[2] Conversion, Calvin argued, is in no way contingent on the functioning of the intellect; it is a suprarational experience brought about by transcendent grace.[3]

Implied by this idea is a split between the divine and the temporal realms, a notion further manifested in the Calvinistic understanding of nature. Nature, separated from the spiritual world by an unbridgeable gap, is a place of deception and the instrument of the devil. Reflecting this attitude toward the world George Herbert, for example, wished to be rescued from the brackish waters of life and from the blister of the flesh, to be pulled up into heaven by a "silk twist." Though, to be fair, Herbert is not strictly a Calvinist in this regard, such a desire emphasizes a dualism in which heaven is wholly separate from and transcendent to earth. For the Calvinist, reason and nature are not *vital* agents for God's administration of divine grace.

Despite the influence of Calvin on his thought, Edward Taylor also affirmed an older, more humanistic tradition. He maintained, as an heir of Augustinian thought, a respect for the rational faculty and a high regard for nature, and we commence this study of Taylor's verse with a review of these two issues. Specifically, this chapter concerns four kindred ideas stemming from the poet's psychological and theological beliefs: (1) human reason, (2) nature and its relation to reason, (3) the effects of the Fall on reason and nature, and (4) faith. It is important to reconsider these four tenets in order to discern several premises on which Taylor's verse is structured. An understanding of them and their Augustinian heritage is cardinal to the subsequent

2. It has been suggested by Herschel Baker that Calvin sought to depose the humanist tradition and its emphasis on reason (*The Wars of Truth: Studies in the Decay of Christian Humanism in the Earlier Seventeenth Century*, p. 100).

3. John Calvin, *Institutes of the Christian Religion*, trans. Ford L. Battles, 3.2.

chapters, which discuss Taylor's quest for conversion and the effect of this search on the thought and techniques of the *Preparatory Meditations*.

i

Taylor's conception of reason—he also refers to it as *understanding, discretion*, and *intellect*—closely resembles that of "traditional" Puritan thought. Described as the eye of the soul,[4] this faculty was chiefly identified by Puritan divines as the primary locus of the divine image. Its foundation was believed to lie in the Son of God, who was thought to be the paradigm of all rationality and "in whom all the Springs of reason rise" (C, p. 161). When, in Adam, reason contemplated truth, it reflected an image of God's loveliness. Ever since the Fall the rational faculty to some degree shares in divine wisdom whenever it grasps fragments of this truth,[5] for despite its fallen condition this faculty naturally inclines toward God. It innately seeks the divine light of truth which God has revealed through what Taylor calls "Created Wisdom": "Created Wisdom is that light that is Seated in the Intellectuall Faculty filling the Eye of the Soul with a Cleare Sight into all things that are the proper Objects thereof" (C, p. 122).

In Christian tradition truth and wisdom are attributed to the Son of God. In a vivid passage from one of his sermons, Taylor expounds on this point: "Solomons Sight was made thro' muddie Crackt glasses of defiled nature, and therefore tho' it might See deeper thro' the Sides of naturall Corpuscles, than other mere

4. Augustine concluded that sight far excels the other physical senses (*The Trinity*, trans. Stephen McKenna, in *The Fathers of the Church*, 11.1.1, and *On Free Choice of the Will*, trans. Anna S. Benjamin and L. H. Hackstaff, 2.6.53). In his discussion of metaphor, Henry Peacham comments that since the eyes are the least deceived of the senses, they are close to the faculty of reason in this respect (*The Garden of Eloquence*, p. 4). Samuel Willard similarly remarked that the understanding is to serve as man's eyes, that "a thing is so far known, as it is irradiated upon the understanding of the person knowing. As there is not sight actual, but by bringing of the thing seen, to the thing seeing; for which reason, the Object is said to be in the eye: so it is in respect to the Understanding, which is the eye of the mind" (*A Compleat Body of Divinity*, p. 41; also p. 211).

5. See Augustine, *On Free Choice of the Will*, 2.13.142.

5

men; yet the wisdom that is fisht in these rivers, and brought in with it unto the Intellectuall treasury, was but foggy, and fragmentous, in comparison to that which Christs holy Soule was fortified withall. It was pure light Without any Scrap of darkness. Bright Sunshine without any never so small a cloud" (C, p. 208). Christ evinces an "Attractive Efficacy" which draws men to Him not "as the Load Stone draws iron to it, nor as the North Pole, the Needle touched with a Magnet" but through human "Rationall Desires"; for man is more than "an insensible lump of Elements" (C, p. 127). Because Christ encompasses that wisdom which is the ultimate end of all human knowledge, man's intellect evidences an inherent affinity or love for Him (2.158, 62–63). This idea underlies Taylor's requests that Christ "feed" his soul's eye (2.56, 55); reason hungers for the radical food of wisdom and truth: "Draw out thy Wisdom. Wisdoms Crown give mee" (2.14, 44). The merest fraction of this wisdom contributes to an illumination of the faculty of understanding, and with new insight the recipient realizes, as Taylor notes in his comment on Solomon, that in comparison to Christ's Truth, "Humane Wisdom's hatcht within the nest / Of addle brains which wisdom ne'er possesst" (2.95, 11–12), that "man's Wisdom up doth rise / Like Childrens catching speckled Butterflies" (2.37, 11–12).

In regard to the question of how reason attains wisdom, Taylor relied on the Augustinian view of the cognate relation between intellectual and sensible knowledge.[6] This concept, pre-

6. See Augustine, *The Teacher*, trans. Joseph M. Colleran, in *Ancient Christian Writers*, 12.39 and *The Trinity*, 15.12.21. This issue is less certain in many medieval inheritors of his thought, but by intellectual knowledge Augustine did not mean Plato's theory of memory. For him intellectual knowledge referred less to a reservoir of innate ideas than to an interior light, capacity, teacher, or principle which, though not itself derived from experience, responds to and gives meaning to experiental learning; through sensible knowledge (*scientia*) man proceeds toward wisdom (*sapientia*) (*The Trinity*, 13.19.24).

That Puritan divines encountered difficulty in explaining these two modes of knowing is clear from Perry Miller's discussion of their effort to distinguish sensory knowledge from that of the interior principle (*New England Mind*, 1: 193–94). In "A Man of Reason" (MS, 1709), Cotton Mather tries to resolve the problem by reasserting Augustine's interpretation. Reason, Mather explains, possesses seminal principles implanted in it by God. These inherently conform to the divine will and are stimulated by sensory experience

serving the Scholastic respect for the body's senses (the subject of the next chapter), may have informed Taylor's distinction between the inward and outward principles of reason (TCLS, p. 61). But it is certainly evident in his distinction between saving and common knowledge. Common knowledge, associated with the external principle of the understanding, stems from perception, that is, from the senses. It is available to any rational creature, indeed even to Satan, who "as an Eaves dropper gets the knowledge of what is said in the house" (C, p. 369). For the saint, the basic value of the scientific truth he perceives from his sensory encounters with natural phenomena lies in its quickening of his "naturall Conscience" to an awareness of the degradation of sin.[7] However, saving knowledge, as opposed to common knowledge, is identified by Taylor with the internal principle of reason, whereby the mind perceives through itself. Saving knowledge is the product of grace and it transforms the soul into "a Child of Light"; by means of it the soul "is renewed in the image of God" (C, p. 370). It is this saving knowledge which provides a sure foundation for true spiritual meditation, an observation readily ascertained from Taylor's *Preparatory Meditations*.

Adam, of course, originally possessed both kinds of wisdom. In fact, it was owing to his saving knowledge that he immediately knew the proper names of the animals (C, pp. 208–9). But as a result of Adam's Fall from grace, mankind is bereft of such truth and wisdom; and to Adam's descendants common knowledge even often *seems* to be diametrically opposed to saving wisdom. Common knowledge has become so miserably obscure that now the "bodies Eyes are blind, no sight therein / Is Cleare enough" (2.147, 31–32).

(see Miller, *New England Mind*, 2: 426–27).

7. For Willard common knowledge activates the "inward senses." The imagination or fancy, he wrote, receives images and impressions of things as they are conveyed by the body's "outward senses." The business of synthesizing whatever is presented to the imagination belongs to the "cogitation." It is the function of memory, however, to retain what the cogitation has communicated to it as well as to release this stored information to the fancy when the occasion requires (*A Compleat Body of Divinity*, p. 120). See also John Cotton, *The Way of Life*, pp. 97–98.

Yet man's ability to discern truth can be enlivened. With the initiation of the regenerative process by Christ's grace, "the internall Eye Sight" of reason becomes partially enlightened. Then it can again begin to reintegrate common and saving wisdom. Hence reason will again partially perceive the "glorious light the Sin blind Eye doth miss" (2.147, 34).

Taylor examined this prelude to the experience of conversion in the writing of his diarylike meditations. There, in response to the penetration of Christ's bright arrows of wisdom—which, as common knowledge, continually pierce through the "Casement of Senses: Reason's Chancery" (2.36, 4)—the poet's "mentall Eye" devotedly conducted "an inward Search" (2.27, 1–6). For Taylor, as for many other Puritan divines, the understanding, albeit not the central faculty, was certainly a fundamental cornerstone in the experience of conversion. Grace enables this faculty to derive from saving and common knowledge a harmonious rational vision. Indeed, were he unable to regulate his body and soul, his whole being, Taylor would be out of tune with the inward principle of his intellect, a point to be considered in detail in the third chapter. His mind would then remain predisposed to its distorted perception of common knowledge. He would, as a result, time and again fail to subordinate lesser things to more important ones, for he would lack right reason.[8] And, as Taylor knew, without right reason, he must stand outside the City of God.

ii

Although he was concerned more with human nature than with natural phenomena, Taylor held that they were closely related. For him nature (a) bears a radical affiliation with its Creator;

---

8. See Augustine, *The Advantage of Believing*, trans. Luanne Meagher, in *The Fathers of the Church*, 12.27, and *On Free Choice of the Will*, 3.5.61. For more information on the nature of right reason, see Robert Hoopes, *Right Reason in the English Renaissance* and William G. Madsen, "The Idea of Nature in Milton's Poetry," *Three Studies in the Renaissance: Sidney, Jonson, Milton*, p. 240.

(b) partakes of the order of grace; and (c) reveals, as God's agent, the divine will.

(a) Because it was created through the spoken art of his son—"Creation in Generall is an Externall Worke of God, whereby God hath made all things of nothing by the word of his Power"[9]—nature evidences God's aesthetic design. As the expression of the Logos, it reflects the divine image.[10] This is what Taylor wished to see in nature:

> Lord, let thy Dazzling Shine refracted fan'de
>   In this bright Looking Glass, its favour lay
> Upon mine Eyes that oculated stand
>   And peep thereat, in button moulds of clay.
>
> $(2.9, 1-4)$[11]

To argue that nature bears the divine image does not necessarily imply a pantheistic view of God. Taylor, consciously avoiding such an heretical notion, adhered to Augustinian reasoning for the *ex nihilo* origin of the universe, arguments which refute any idea of God's spatial or actual presence in nature.[12] Through his word, God "spake all things from nothing; and with ease / Can speake all things to nothing"; He "All from Nothing fet, from Nothing, All: / Hath All on Nothing set, lets Nothing fall" (GD, pp. 387–88).

This view did not, however, prevent Taylor from maintaining another Augustinian notion: that nature shares something with its Creator. Nature does not merely reflect an image of His loveliness and declare His incomparable righteousness (TCLS, p.

9. Westfield "Church Record" (MS, Edwin Smith Historical Museum, Westfield Athenaeum), p. 16.

10. In his miscellanies Edwards wrote: "the Son of God created the world for this very end, to communicate Himself in an image of his own excellency," and, therefore, "the beauties of nature are really emanations or shadows of the excellencies of the Son of God" (*Jonathan Edwards: Representative Selections*, ed. Clarence H. Faust and Thomas H. Johnson, rev. ed., p. 373).

11. For a similarly worded passage in another of Taylor's poems, see Donald E. Stanford, "The Giant Bones of Claverack, New York, 1705," *New York History*, 40 (January 1959), 57.

12. See especially Augustine, *Confessions*, trans. R. S. Pine-Coffin, 12.7.

54), but it evidences some real and intimate relation to God:

> What Birth of Wonders from thy Fingers ends
>> Dropt, when the World, Lord, dropt out of the Womb
> Of its Non-Entity.
>
> (2.89, 1–3)

> Life from thy Fingers ends runs, and ore spred
>> Itselfe through all thy Works what e're they bee.
>
> (2.15, 33–34)

It is being or life—"the finest flower in natures garden"; "Natures Principall, that makes all brisk, / Peart, Flowerish, Glorious" (C, p. 191; 2.87, 5–6)—which creation shares with God: "Creation is an Externall Worke peculiarly Proper unto God whereby according to his Decree hee gives being unto all things."[13] To be sure, nature possesses being to a considerably lesser degree than does God; but as Taylor's use of the image of a fluid origin from the Son's hand implies, nature's life, the fact that it has existence at all, unites it in some essential way with its Creator. Nature is imbued with a divine *Aqua Vitae*, with the water of life (i.e., divine love and grace), which endlessly flows from the Creator. It is not surprising, therefore, that love is the central theme of the *Preparatory Meditations*, for God's love is what is communicated to and animates all existence. Without this love, Taylor explains, "no Life's in mee that's worth a Fly" (2.82, 27).

It is important to remember, however, that Taylor never obscures the difference, implicit in his concept of an *ex nihilo* genesis, between God and nature. At times, in fact, he seems almost to have repudiated any such connection between them. On one occasion he explained to his parishioners in simplified terms that "Created Nature and Uncreated nature are Contraries and as it were Contradictories" (C, p. 161). This remark is nevertheless in accord with Augustinian thought in that the church father himself had reasoned how created nature cannot be like divine

13. Westfield "Church Record," p. 15.

nature or else it would be God. Moreover, Taylor worded his assertion strongly in order to impress upon the laity the magnificence of the Incarnation, which is the basic focus of the sermon in which the passage occurs. For Taylor, God's "Being Being gave to all that be" (2.17, 2); and the Incarnation reasserts this genesis, elevating created nature "as nigh to increated Nature as is possible" (c, p. 161). Thus, for Taylor as for Augustine, nature's being shares in God's Being in some fundamental way.[14] Consequently, no aspect of nature can rightly be thought of as contrary to the divine will.

(b) This idea of nature influenced the kindred notions that heaven and earth are essentially united and that even fallen nature partakes of the order of grace. Taylor warned, of course, that since heaven is next to God and earth is next to nothing, one should not seek too close an analogy between the orders of grace and of nature. Nevertheless, he did not discern an unbridgeable gap between them. It was Calvin who, in opposition to the Renaissance concept of man's natural ability to lead a rational Christian life, denigrated the temporal realm and identified grace as wholly transcendent. Calvin's notion fractured an older medieval synthesis found in such writings as those of Augustine. To Augustine, heaven and earth share a common essence. Both were simultaneously created from formless matter or nothing and both are subject to mutability.[15] Furthermore, the progress and proper destiny of the heavenly and earthly orders currently remain mingled, even as they were in Eden.[16] Eden was indeed

14. See Daniel D. Williams, "The Significance of St. Augustine Today" and David E. Roberts, "The Earliest Writings," both in *A Companion to the Study of St. Augustine*, ed. Roy W. Battenhouse, pp. 3–14, 93–126. For Edwards the difference between God and nature "is no contrariety" (Egbert C. Smyth, "Jonathan Edwards' Idealism," *American Journal of Theology*, 1, October 1897, 988). For an opposite interpretation of Taylor's view of nature, see Norman S. Grabo, *Edward Taylor*, p. 45.

15. See Augustine, *Confessions*, 12.7, 17, 19.

16. See Augustine, *The City of God*, trans. Marcus Dods, 11.1, 12.4, 14.2. In his *De Doctrina Christiana*, Milton argues that these two orders are essentially united and incorruptible (*The Student's Milton*, ed. Frank A. Patterson, p. 976). Likewise in *Paradise Lost* nature is said to function in a "harmonie Divine" (5: 625), and Eden attracts the heavenly spirits (5: 372–75). Even perverse Satan is moved to exclaim, "O Earth, how like to Heav'n, if not preferr'd" (9:99). For the influence of Milton on New England

a complete paradise in that the external senses of Adam's body as well as the internal senses of his mind or soul were afforded concurrent enjoyment. Eden, that is to say, satisfied the physical and the spiritual needs of Adam's entire being, provided for the requisites of the whole man.

This was Taylor's view as well. "Earth once was Paradise of Heaven below," and since the Fall Eden has been harbored in "Heav'ns upmost Loft" ("The Reflexion," ll. 19, 22). Taylor perceived no real separation between the spiritual and the temporal realms despite their qualitative difference:

> Thy Lower House, this World well garnished
>   With richest Furniture of Ev'ry kinde
> Of Creatures of each Colours varnished
>   Most glorious, a Silver Box of Winde.
>   The Crystall Skies pinkt with Sun, Moon, and Stars
>   Are made its Battlements on azure Spars.
>
> But on these Battlements above, thoust placdst
>   Thy Upper House, that Royall Palace town,
> In which these Mansions are, that made thou hast
>   For Saints and Angells Dwellings of renown.
>   Should we suppose these mansions, chambers neate
>   Like ours, 't would sordid be, not fit this Seate.
>   (2.93, 13–24)

Both the lower and the upper "houses"—perhaps echoing Augustine's two cities—had a beginning, from which time they have always remained joined. Especially since the Incarnation,

> Life Naturall (although Essentiall to
>   All Living things) and Spirituall Life indeed,
> Peculiar to Rationalls also
>   Containd are in Christs Gift as in a Seed,
>   Are both Adjuncted with Eternity
>   In that he gives them them Eternally.
>   (2.90, 37–42)

Puritans, see George F. Sensabaugh, *Milton in Early America.*

In order to convey this notion of the bond between these two realms, Taylor resorted to metaphorical terms: "Life Naturall's the Base: the Spirituall is / The Meane: The Tenour is Eternal Bliss" (2.90, 59–60). That Taylor should employ metaphor in regard to the natural and spiritual orders is particularly significant to our later discussion of his idea of poetic decorum and of his alleged mysticism.

For Taylor the essential union of heaven and earth is reflected in a chain of being. According to this idea all creation, including heaven as well as earth, is arranged in a harmonious and interlocking hierarchy of sequential stages of being.[17] These stages not only ascend to God, their apex, but their existence depends on him; for his grace or love—that is, his being—provides the central reality and cohesive force underlying and penetrating each of the levels.[18] Taylor refers to this chain both as "the Scale of nature" (C, p. 22; TCLS, p. 101) and as a hierarchy of glory (C, pp. 159–60). This idea informs his association of the spiritual realm with gold—thought to be the most precious of metals—and the temporal realm with silver (2.93, 16–28); but it is even more overt in his portrait of the Logos in the act of creation:

> Life Vegitative now hatcht in the Egge,
>   Flourishing some things nobler than the rest.
> Life sensitive gives some of these its Head,
>   Inspiring them with honour next the best.
> And some of which Life Rationall Enfires,
>   Cloathed with a Spiritualizing Life, aspires.
>
> This Life thy Fingers freely dropt into
>   The Humane shaped Elements and made

17. For a full treatment of this theory, see Arthur O. Lovejoy, *The Great Chain of Being*, 1936.

18. Employing a metaphor which was popular with Puritan divines and which would appear again in the writings of the American Transcendentalists (particularly Whitman), Willard explains: every "Creature is, as it were, a small spring or rivulet of goodness" because it derives its being from God, who is "the vast and boundless Ocean of universal Perfection" (*A Compleat Body of Divinity*, p. 47). Edwards explains this tenet in detail in *Dissertation Concerning the End for Which God Created the World*.

13

The same Excell the Rest and nobler goe
Enspirited with Heavenizing trade.

(2.89, 13–22)

Glory lin'de out a Paradise in Power
Where e'vy seed a Royall Coach became
For Life to ride in, to each shining Flower
And made mans Flower with glory all ore flame.

(1.33, 19–22)

As these preceding lines also suggest, man is the amphibian between the beasts (with their sensitive nature) and the angels (with their intellectual nature). Adam, who "bore the Bell: / Shone like a Carbuncle in Glories Shell" (2.28, 5–6), was, while adorned with glory in his unfallen state, the mirror of God's works (2.30, 7–8). Moreover, the maintenance of Eden's sublimity depended "in an ordinary way" on Adam's glory and on his ability to integrate reason and nature, for he had been appointed by virtue of his position in the scale of nature as God's "Steward to looke to his Creatures and return that revenue of his glory in the Creatures from them in a Rationall way to himselfe" (C, p. 96).

Taylor comments further on this hierarchy of degrees of glory and on man's place in this scheme: "In creation, this hath been the method God hath taken to scatter abroad the streaking beams of His own divine wisdom, viz., to proceed from things less excellent to things more excellent, and to man at last, that all the less perfect things might be but serviters to man the most complete" (TCLS, pp. 142–43). Hence, as the Second Adam, Christ was "th' Creame of Natures top Perfection"; he possessed "all Sorts or Kinds of Life. From the life of a Sweete little Herb, to the Life of an high and Holy Angell" (C, p. 176). Christ, as perfect man, embodied the consummate fusion of the vegetative, sensitive, and rational levels of being.

Implied throughout Taylor's affirmation of a chain of being is the belief that, aside from God, nothing else is content with itself as its own end. Divine Providence engendered in creation an unmitigable sense of incompleteness. "Something that is most

14

concerning, as the *ultima lima* of glory last attained unto, as an allurement unto the most excellent accomplishments in order thereunto" has been held in reserve by God (TCLS, p. 143). Each of the levels in the scale of nature inevitably tends toward the "allurement" or attraction of a more perfect degree of being or grace.[19] For Taylor, therefore, it was not only through the Incarnation that God made "all Conspire / In all their Jars, and Junctures, Good-bad wayes" toward a single, unified end (1.35, 20–21). On the contrary, the Incarnation reemphasized the fact that nature, always reflecting divine goodness, never manifests any inherent tendency toward discord. It participates in the order of grace; and owing to this essential union, "Grace doth not debilitate, or disgrace, but regulate, and exalt the Law of Nature, and improove it, to attend matters not Contrary to, but above the Precepts of the Law of Nature" (c, p. 31).[20] Every motion is upheld by, inclined toward, and resolved in the very source of its origin: the greatest good, God's love.

(c) Creation, rooted and conserved in being or love by the

19. Nature was to be spiritualized, man was to join the angels, and perhaps even the angels were destined to some sort of change (see Augustine, *City of God*, 12.15.21). Adam was slated for an eventual transformation. Though he was "a fit Subject of Compleate Beauty as to matter and Form" and though he was initially free from fault, "Yet perhaps there might be Something deficient as to degrees. Hee might, so far as we know, have grown bigger" (c, p. 247). Taylor indicated that Adam's growth was to be of a spiritual as well as of a physical nature: "Grace in Adam, tho' it was so in him as it never was in any again, Christ only excepted . . . was to attain to its perfection by growth: and that both in respect unto its extent over his Actions and life, and in respect unto its intensness, or Degrees" (c, p. 244). However, in spite of these remarks, Taylor apparently remained somewhat uncertain of this argument (see c, p. 445). Willard endorsed it: Adam "was *fitted for* happiness, inasmuch as he had all that stock of Grace put into his hands, which was sufficient by improvement to make him happy" (*A Compleat Body of Divinity*, p. 11).

20. The normal course of God's wisdom as demonstrated "through the whole scale of nature" is "to use such things to produce such effects as having a suitableness in their nature unto such effects"(TCLS, p. 101). The reception of grace, it follows, is an event in nature. God treats men as men: "we are in the way of ordinary dispensations, and therefore are not to expect extraordinary communications" (TCLS, p. 157). God converts men in the immediacy of their daily lives, and often his spiritual influences are conveyed through such physical channels as the beauties of nature. Hence Taylor responds appropriately to nature's "perfumes pufft out from Pincks, and Roses" with thoughts of Christ, "A Pillar of Perfume" (1.3, 9, 14).

15

Son—the Logos literally speaks again and again[21]—inherently turns back to the provenance of all life. Since it reflects the divine image of love and glory back to God and since it is "Adjuncted with Eternity," nature always leans toward God.[22] What is implied here is a circular movement from God to nature and then from nature back to God, a movement to be considered in the light of Taylor's poetic decorum in chapter 5. In response to the inherent impulse of its being, "Creation doth bring all its Shining Glory, as a Sacrifice to be offerd up to God" (C, p. 312). Thus, in one poem Taylor rebukes himself for wasting his love on phenomenal matters and for failing to perceive the underlying meaning of all creation: "Nature's amaz'de, Oh monstrous thing Quoth shee, / Not Love my life?" (1.33, 13–14). Nature, speaking clearly, points beyond herself to the very essence of her being; she thereby indicts the persona of the poem for failing to appreciate the animating source of her being as well as of his own: Life itself, which is God, whose "Being Being gave to all that be."[23]

Owing to this circular movement, nature becomes God's agent. It communicates the divine will, the power of which, as

21. Edwards, speaking of this concept, argues that at every second nature participates wholly and really in the Word's continuous and immediate reassertion of its life or being: "All dependent existence whatsoever is in a constant flux, ever passing and returning; renewed every moment . . . ; and all is constantly proceeding from God, as light from the sun" (*Original Sin*, ed. Clyde A. Holbrook, p. 404). See also Douglas J. Elwood, *The Philosophical Theology of Jonathan Edwards*, pp. 28–36.

22. See Augustine, *Confessions*, 13.2. Christopher O'Toole has explained that for Augustine the formation of nature "does not appear to result in the insertion of independent forms in created matter, but rather leads us back to the source of being. From that source there streams forth an illumination which keeps the creatures formed. From the creature's point of view this will imply a constant *conversio* toward the source of light" (*The Philosophy of Creation in the Writings of Saint Augustine*, p. 105).

23. Citing this poem may raise difficulties of interpretation. The poem has been read as Taylor's reflection on his wife's death (July 7, 1689), an interpretation I have never found convincing. It is clear that the language, motifs, development, and argument of the poem do not differ significantly from those of the other meditations. It may also be argued that even if Taylor intended double entendre, at which he is indeed proficient, then the theological aspect of the poem, the aspect I stress above, is allowable. See also Stanford, "Two Notes on Edward Taylor," p. 92.

the "Cradle" of creation (2.89, 3–4), "runs its Efficacie thro' the Whole Scale of Nature, from the Highest Angell in Heaven thro' all the ranks of Creatures to the Smalest mite" (C, p. 220; see also pp. 10, 378–79, 454). Creation is a book, complementary in later times to that of Scripture, wherein man can discover, through the art of the Logos, Providence's eternal decrees.[24] Like Adam, all men are obliged to exercise reason in order to read nature; they are to respond properly to what is divinely revealed there and are circularly to move closer to God. In "Upon a Wasp Child with Cold," for instance, Taylor explains that even in an insect man can

> A school and a schoolmaster see
> Where we may learn, and easily finde
> A nimble Spirit bravely minde
> Her worke in e'ry limb.

This is part of God's plan. After the creation of the world, he "Plac'de man his Pupill here, and ev'ry thing, / With loads of Learning, came to tutor him" (2.41, 5–6).

For Taylor, therefore, natural law reflects God's rational design. Since it manifests the divine image, nature is permeated with the "sweet harmony of reason" (TCLS, p. 43). The law of nature and the law of reason are in fact one and the same; both bear the divine image and both point to the same ultimate truth. Consequently, in man's regenerate state, scientific or common knowledge, sensually garnered from the world, conforms to and is reinforced by intellectual or saving knowledge, imprinted upon the soul as innate principles. Taylor, in brief, believed that man should use reason, with the aid of biblical illumination, to comprehend and appreciate the revelation of God's will in nature.

24. In "the *book of nature*, the great and admirable works of God," explains Willard, "there is never a leaf . . . but hath something of God written legibly upon it, and many Characters of his Divine power, wisdom, and goodness there engraven" (*A Compleat Body of Divinity*, p. 34).

At the decisive moment in Eden, Adam sinned when he failed to exercise right reason and obey the law of nature. Taylor's portrait of how Satan tempts the elect in *Gods Determinations* intimates that sin often occurs when man does not rationally perceive the proper meaning of nature. Hence, recapitulating how he foiled Adam and Eve, Satan directs his current assaults upon man's understanding and ultimately upon his heart or will through the senses of the body while they are engaged in nature, the realm of common knowledge:

> Hence in their joy he straweth poyson on,
> Those Objects that their senses feed upon.
> By some odde straggling thought up poyson flies
> Into the heart: and through the Eares, and Eyes.
> Which sick, lies gasping: Other thoughts then high
> To hold its head; and Venom'd are thereby.
>
> (GD, pp. 406–7)

As a consequence of the poisonous infection of sin, Adam

> did at the threashould trip
> Fell, Crackt the glass through which the Sun
> should shine
> That darkness gross his noble Soule doth tip.
>
> (2.41, 7–9)

The glass Adam shattered was, of course, his soul's eye, the rational faculty which had previously mirrored God's image of divine love. Adam, deficient in his love for God, broke the golden box of intellect, which had previously been inlaid with truth and wisdom and which now is filled with the dross of falsehood (2.50, 10–12). All of Adam's descendants are likewise "Bereav'd of Reason"; deprived of saving knowledge, "the Reasonable Soule doth much delight / A Pickpack t'ride o'th'Sensuall Appitite" (GD, pp. 389, 409). Now man attributes goodness to evil and iniquity to good, for his "Wits run a Wooling" (1.29, 2), his

18

"thoughts are Laberryntht," continually "brambled in the briers of [the] minde" (GD, p. 442) and "in Snick-Snarls run" (1.25, 16). As a result of sin man's rational faculty has been transformed:

> The Scull without, not fring'd with Wisdom fleece.
> The pan within a goose pen full of geese.
>
> There Reason's wick yarn-like ore twisted Snarles
>   Chandled with Sensuall tallow out doth blaze
> A smoaky flame upon its hurden harles
>   That Wil-a-Wisps it into boggy wayes.
>
> (2.45, 5–10)

Nevertheless, as these preceding lines indicate, the light of reason, while considerably diminished and obscured by the deprivation of God's illumination, is not totally extinguished. A vestigial love of truth persists, and man is to use his intellect, in spite of its dimness, to the best of his ability. Though he gropes in the dark, man must, with the aid of the Bible, exercise his purblind rational eye and struggle to comprehend the natural world in order to derive some insight into God's will.

Just as reason's reflection of the divine image is not wholly obliterated, that of nature likewise persists. At first this observation may seem specious, especially in the light of what sometimes appears to be Taylor's condemnation of postlapsarian nature as a possible corrupt influence on man. In these instances what Taylor means, I think, is not applicable to the essential goodness at the core of nature. Taylor is very clear that God cannot be frustrated in a single design or thought by any creature, whether he be a wicked man or a fallen angel. Sin, as we shall see more fully in chapter 3, proves insufficient to thwart the plan of creation. It follows, therefore, that since nature is conserved in being and is at every moment reasserted by its Creator, it continues to manifest a radical goodness, thereby remaining an agent of the divine Will.

The logical corollary to this tenet, for Taylor as for Augustine, is that blame cannot be ascribed to anything which man misuses or adversely affects. Culpability lies solely with the moral agent.

It is man's act of sinning, not its apparent effects on nature, which is contrary to God.[25] It is understandable, therefore, why in one of his meditations Taylor humbly presents nature as worthier of divine attention than is mankind: "Pritty Bird, Flower, Star or Shining Sun, / Poure out o'reflowing Glory"; "all this Glory to my Lord's a spot / While I instead of any, am all blot" (1.25, 14–18). Even after man's Fall, nature maintains her beauty, glorifies God, and continues to participate in the order of grace.

But, subsequent to the Fall, natural phenomena appear distorted to man. Man's depraved state isolates him to the extent that he no longer contributes to or clearly perceives nature's underlying harmony. Because of human sin nature can scarcely give man "life enough, to let him feel he lives" (GD, p. 390); man has been deprived of degrees of being or divine love. Hence, speaking as an Adamic everyman, Taylor laments:

> But as a Chrystall Glass, I broke, and lost
>   That Grace, and Glory I was fashion'd in
> And cast this Rosy World with all its Cost
>   Into a Dunghill Pit, and Puddle Sin.
>   All right I lost in all Good things, each thing
>   I had did hand a Vean of Venom in.
>
> (1.31, 7–12)

To fallen man's clouded rational sight physical phenomena become delusive; they seem to align themselves with his distorted affections. It is in this sense that the course of nature has been corrupted and subsequently "doth in its naturall order produce Corrupt fruite" (C, p. 23). Man, as the crown of creation, has "undone the World" (2.35, 39) in that *for him* the beauty of nature is "Poysond" (2.27, 13), "saddlebackt with Loads of Sin" (2.29, 3), and transformed into a "dirty slough / We puddle in below and Wallow now" (2.138, 5–6). For fallen man creation takes on a vicious appearance; no longer does *natura naturata* readily reveal to him its harmonious union with *natura naturans*.

---

25. See Augustine, *City of God*, 12.3. Calvin taught that man's depravity did not originate in nature (*Institutes*, 3.9.1). Similarly in *Paradise Lost* nature is innocent of man's Fall, though it suffers some effects (9: 782–89, 1000–4).

By his sin natural phenomena "were pulld asunder, and made to jar, and clash" (C, p. 303), and now to his perverted perception "nature's vineyard is all run over with nettles and brambles" (TCLS, p. 26).

With saving knowledge, however, one can recognize this distortion and discern nature's fundamental goodness. What the nettles and brambles of *natura naturata* can provide for the person with grace is a regenerating purgative process:

> Each twig is bow'd with loads of follies Rhime.
> That ev'ry thing in tutoring, is a toole
> To whip the Scholler that did play the foole.
>
> (2.41, 10–12)

Taylor, unlike John Donne, did not usually emphasize this aspect of divine Providence. Yet, upon occasion he certainly interpreted Christ's redemption of man in terms of purgation, as in the following echo of Romans 8: 22:

> Our Nature spoild: under all Curses groans
>   Is purg'd, tooke, grac'd with grace, united to
> A Godhead person.
>
> (2.44, 31–33)

Christ's Incarnation, as the following chapter will argue, reconciles heaven and earth in that it reasserts or re-creates the fundamental and inviolable union of the orders of nature and grace.

To perceive this harmony with true insight—not sensuously or mystically, but rationally—depends on the illumination of the intellect by grace:

> This Curious pearle, One Syllable, call'd LIFE,
>   That all things struggle t'keep, and we so prize
> I'd with the Edge of sharpen'd sight (as knife)
>   My understanding sheath'th anatomize
>   But finde Life far too fine, I can not know't.
>   My sight too Dull; my knife's too blunt to do't.
>
> (2.80, 1–6)[26]

26. See also Cotton, *The Way of Life*, p. 274.

Hence, Taylor's poetry abounds with requests for the renewal of his understanding: "enoculate within mine Eye / Thy Image bright" (2.59, 1–2); "give my Souls Cleare Eye of thee a Sight / As thou shinst its bright looking Glasses bright" (2.125, 5–6). Such entreaties arose from Taylor's recognition of the significance of the awakening of reason in the drama of conversion. God converts or turns men away from sin and toward Himself primarily through the instrumental faculties of the soul: "He useth the exercise of their own understanding, conscience, judgment and wills: and the manner of His proceeding this way is by enlightening of them, convicting of them, and so turning the heart" (TCLS, p. 99).[27]

This enlightenment does not result in a new faculty but in an awakening of the intellect and in the partial restoration of the divine image. Grace reinvigorates the internal and external principles of reason, commencing the restoration of the faculty to its proper hierarchical relation to the senses. Though they are never fully renovated in the temporal world, the rational powers of the saint contribute to the collective intellect of the church, which bears the "flaming Torch of Grace" (2.135, 7–8).

iv

Of all the gifts of grace, faith is the most precious. In *The First Principles* James Fitch, Taylor's father-in-law, makes the following observation about reason and faith: "Reason in a believer is a means to let in a light and good beyond Reason, that as the senses are means to present Reason in things to the Reason of man, although Reason is above Sense, so Reason is a means to present a divine good unto Faith, though that divine good is above Reason."[28] Taylor similarly maintained this conservative

27. In *A Divine and Supernatural Light* Edwards, who differs significantly from Taylor concerning the drama of conversion, similarly held that "God, in letting in this light into the soul, deals with man according to his nature, or as a rational creature; and makes use of his human faculties" (*The Works of President Edwards*, 4: 443). See also his *Religious Affections*, p. 206.

28. *The First P[r]inciples of the Doctrine of Christ*, p. 4. In *Errand into the Wilderness* Perry

view. Faith never instructs contrary to right reason; in fact, right reason depends on and inclines toward faith:

> The Christian Faith cannot abide at least
>> To dash out reasons brains, or blinde its eye.
>> Faith never blindeth reasons Eye but cleares
>> Its Sight to see things quite above its Sphere.
>
> (2.108, 27–30)

The saint's rational thoughts will be "Well splic'de with Saving Faith" (2.94, 8).

"Faiths round appled Eye" enables the "Souls peirt Eye" to display glory (2.125, 19–20). Taylor rarely portrayed faith as an overwhelming force; it never supplants the intellect. It is a revitalization of the understanding, a

> Light, Ophthalmicks pure
>> To heate my Eyes and make the Sight the Quicker.
>> That I may use Sins Spectacles no more.
>
> (2.67 [B], 56–58)

"Sins Spectacles" are replaced by those of faith, and the saint's rational vision becomes clearer than previously:

> Mine Eyes are dim; I cannot clearly see.
> Be thou my Spectacles that I may read
>> Thine Image, and Inscription stampt on mee.
>
> (1.6, 8–10)

> Although thy Love play bow-peep with me here.
> Though I be dark: want Spectacles to prove
>> Thou lovest mee: I shall at last see Clear.
>
> (2.96, 50–52)

Whereas the eye of the soul inherently seeks the expression of

---

Miller cites John Preston: "Faith addeth to the eye of reason, and raiseth it higher" (p. 80).

God's will in postlapsarian nature, it can, when assisted by the glasses of faith, spontaneously move toward the more enlightened revelation of that will in Scripture. The Bible reveals more clearly what the book of nature obscurely teaches. Before the Bible, natural law guided man (Rom. 2:14), an observation which permitted Christian-humanist thinkers and their Puritan heirs to find truth and wisdom in the writings of certain pagan authors.[29] However, "The Creatures field no food for Souls e're gave" (1.8, 14), by which Taylor means, among other things, that the law of nature is insufficient to save man.[30] Scripture provides the key to a saving knowledge of the divine will.

The Bible was indeed for Taylor the object of faith and the measure of reason. Like faith, Scripture is always in accord with right reason (TCLS, p. 159), and it is man's nature that he must be instructed in the twofold manner of reason and authority.[31] When reason fails, he must turn to the authority of faith and Scripture. "Faith will stand where Reason hath no ground" (GD, p. 436). In matters "whose root / Too deep's for reasons delving toole to finde" (2.105, 9–10), reason should faithfully submit to the authority of Holy Writ. In the drama of conversion faith, right reason, and natural law collectively instruct the saint in the love of God.

Underlying the thought, imagery, and conception of decorum in Edward Taylor's *Preparatory Meditations* is this perception of the harmony between Scripture, reason, and nature. Taylor held, as did many other early Puritan divines, that the experience of

---

29. See Richard M. Gummere, *The American Colonial Mind and the Classical Tradition.*

30. In the Westminster Confession of Faith it is written that "although the light of nature, and the works of creation and providence, do so far manifest the goodness, wisdom, and power of God, as to leave men inexcusable; yet are they not sufficient to give that knowledge of God, and his will, which is necessary unto salvation" (*The Creeds of Christendom*, ed. Philip Schaff, 1.1). (At the time of Westfield's foundation of a formal church in 1679, Taylor, to the disapproval of neighboring ministers, had planned to substitute the Westminster Confession for a personal statement of the principal tenets of his faith.) Willard similarly reasoned that nature leaves "a man short of the saving knowledge of [God]; there is enough there for man's Condemnation, but not for their Salvation" (*A Compleat Body of Divinity*, p. 34).

31. See Augustine, *Divine Providence and the Problem of Evil*, trans. Robert P. Russell, in *The Fathers of the Church*, 2.9.26.

24

conversion and the ensuing process of regeneration affect both the internal and external principles of the understanding. Saving grace urges the saint's newly illuminated rational faculty to perceive the divine truth mutually manifested by Scripture and nature. It is the "inward Search" for this enlightened assent and its vital influence on the will (to be discussed in chapter 3) which partly characterize Taylor's quest for conversion in his meditations.

v

As the years passed and the ideals of their society glimmered in the waning light of their numerous jeremiads, conservative Puritans such as Taylor had to contend with an increasing number of factions threatening to splinter this synthesis of Scripture, reason, and nature. The problem had apparently existed from the beginning of the New England experiment, and perhaps there never was in the strictest sense a synthesis at all. But clearly such ministers must have sensed that a former unity was dissolving; for in spite of the fact that the New Lights generally did not entirely dismiss the role of reason in conversion, they did seek to counter what they construed to be the Old Light's exaggerated stress on this faculty.[32] Already by 1720, moreover, New England was feeling the effects of burgeoning deistic notions emerging from changing scientific methods and widening philosophical concerns. No less a brilliant mind than that of Jonathan Edwards, in an effort to keep Puritanism alive, would wrestle with the problem of reasserting the older view of the unity of nature and Scripture.

We can conclude from what has survived of his writings that in the midst of the encroaching tenets of the New Lights and the turbulent theological and political disputes in Boston, Taylor's orthodoxy withstood most of the issues raging outside his frontier

---

32. See Richard L. Bushman's informative *From Puritan to Yankee: Character and the Social Order in Connecticut, 1690–1765*. The expression *Old Light* is applied to those orthodox Puritan divines who opposed the revivalism and its related heresies advanced by a younger, more radical generation of divines, the New Lights.

retreat at Westfield. He had joyed in Oliver Cromwell's rule and in King William's revolution of 1688; he had detested the despotic royal governor Sir Edmund Andros and Andros's agent Edward Randolph; he, as well, resisted the rise of Presbyterianism and particularly took vigorous exception to Solomon Stoddard's interpretation of the Lord's Supper.[33] In Westfield he led a conservative Puritan life and preached formal Puritan dogma. There he daily sought what Jonathan Edwards would later describe as Christ's peace, "a reasonable peace and rest of soul; it is what has its foundation in light and knowledge, in the proper exercises of reason, and a right view of things."[34] The enlightened understanding, fortified by grace, engenders a more peaceful state of mind and enables the saint to lead a more rationally governed life. Yet Taylor realized, as did Augustine, that though a man may in fact be "a Child of Light," the drama of conversion is progressive; the wisdom he attains is, in comparison to that of Christ, always "Like Childrens catching speckled Butterflies." Indeed, this very deficiency drives him to God and, with divine mercy, to eternal life, when he will "at last see Clear."

33. See Donald E. Stanford, "Edward Taylor versus the 'Young Cockerill' Benjamin Ruggles: A Hitherto Unpublished Episode from the Annals of Early New England Church History," *New England Quarterly*, 44 (September 1971), 459–68; Stanford, "Edward Taylor and the Lord's Supper," *American Literature*, 27 (May 1955), 172–78; Norman S. Grabo, "Edward Taylor on the Lord's Supper," *Boston Public Library Quarterly*, 12 (January 1960), 22–36; Grabo, "The Poet to the Pope: Edward Taylor to Solomon Stoddard," *American Literature*, 32 (May 1960), 197–201; and Grabo, " 'The Appeale Tried': Another Edward Taylor Manuscript," *American Literature*, 34 (November 1962), 394–400.

34. "The Peace Which Christ Gives His True Followers," *Works*, 4: 434. In his discussion of "the interplay of ideas and feelings in Puritans," Robert Middlekauff concludes that there existed a "pre-eminence of the intellect in Puritan mind and character" ("Piety and Intellect in Puritanism," *William and Mary Quarterly*, 22, July 1965, 457–70).

Chapter II

Like a Golden Lanthorn Grim

THE HUMAN BODY

Too often New England Puritan writings have been read in the light of a Platonic or a stoical conception of the human body. It is true that their sermons and diaries focus on the necessity of restraining the body's unruly appetites and passions. According to their psychology, however, the corrupted flesh actually represents a symptom or sign of sin, a view which does not deem the body as the root of evil and the locus of sinfulness. Puritan divines generally refer to the body in a manner similar to their use of the term *nature*; in both instances they primarily stress the *fallen condition* of nature and the body in order to confront sin in its most evident manifestation, that is to say, in the daily lives of their parishioners. A consideration of their Augustinian and Scholastic heritage, with its respect for the human body, argues in fact for a more integrated conception of the body and the soul.

Edward Taylor did not affirm the Platonic belief that the union of flesh and spirit results in discomfort and harm to the soul, which, as a prisoner of the body, longs to return to its heavenly abode. Nor did he advocate the suppression of the body's senses and affections as a prerequisite for a rational life. As we observed in the last chapter, his belief in God's emanation of degrees of perfection or glory counters any idea of a dualism or dichotomy between the natural (flesh) and the heavenly (spirit) orders. As the link between animals and angels, as the very center and crown of creation, man was destined to use his body as an instrument of his soul.

Furthermore, Taylor had learned from Christian writings such as those of Augustine that the flesh is not inherently wicked.[1] Because in Adam it abided in "the Covenant of Life" (c, p. 116), the human body must share to some degree in the divine Being and therefore must, like everything else in creation, be free from any inherent inclination toward evil. Nevertheless, it could and does suffer from the dire aftermath of sin. But the effect of sin on the body is similar to that on nature; both maintain their essential innocence and beauty. Despite its present fallen state, the human body is still ordained to play an important role in the salvation of the saint.

In order to consider his idea of poetic decorum and the issue of his alleged mysticism, Taylor's view of man's body requires attention. First of all, from the time of its creation by God, the flesh, as the complement of the soul, has been a part of the whole man. Its senses and affections are, consequently, significant to Taylor's search for conversion and his poetic expression of this quest. When he refers to his soul as a "Bird of Paradise put in / This Wicker Cage (my Corps) to tweedle praise" (1.8, 7–8), the poet is suggesting that a close relation exists between his words and the harmonious integration of his body and spirit, a point taken up in the fourth chapter. He further contended that this original design was reasserted by the Incarnation and will be fulfilled by the elect in heaven, where the body of saints, and by synecdoche each saintly body, will be "like a golden Lanthorn trim / Through which the lamps of Grace shine from within."

1. Taylor's "Commonplace Book" (MS, Massachusetts Historical Society, Boston) includes some pertinent items.

For Taylor the human body is the worthy and necessary counterpart of the soul in the drama of conversion.

i

In Puritan thought the body serves the soul by means of its senses and affections. Regarding the former, Puritan divines maintained, as already noted, the Scholastic conviction that reason depends on sensation for scientific knowledge. There is a harmony in this relationship, for the rational soul (reason and will) was thought to be both the animating source and the proper end of the senses. In other words, sensation, as a divinely sanctioned manner of encountering God, arises from the interpenetration of flesh and spirit.[2] Although they always serve the soul in this capacity, the senses were less influential in Adam than they are in his descendants because Adam possessed more of an inward light or, in Taylor's terms, saving knowledge.[3] Since the Fall, however, the proper hierarchical relationship between the two has been subverted and the faculties of the soul now remain largely dependent on the flesh.

Whereas sensation provides *means* for the soul, affections—those modes of response to sensations and ideas—represent *outlets* for the spirit. Generally understood to include passions, appetites, and desires (despite the often pejorative context given these words), the affections are good when rightly exercised. Edward Reynolds, developing an idea similar to Taylor's distinction between the external and internal principles of reason, separated the affections into sensitive and rational passions: "*Sensitive Passions* are those motions of Persecutions or flight, which are grounded on the *Fancie, Memory*, and Apprehensions of the *common Sense*: which we see in *brute beasts*"; "*Rationall*" passions, on the other hand, manifest a "*participation* and *dependance* by reason of their immediate subordination in man unto the government of

2. Augustine, *The Greatness of the Soul*, trans. Joseph M. Colleran, in *Ancient Christian Writers*, 33.71; *City of God*, 13.6.

3. See also Edward Reynolds, *A Treatise of the Passions and Faculties of the Soul of Man*, p. 3. Miller has observed that Reynolds was the only Puritan to have written directly on faculty psychology (*New England Mind*, 1: 244).

the *Will* and *Understanding*, and not barely of the *Fancie.*"[4]

Jonathan Edwards also differentiated between the soul's affections and the body's motions. Though he saw the soul as the only proper seat of the affections, he was careful to make explicit the union existing between the rational faculties and the body. The motions of the animal spirits and bodily fluids are distinct from the soul's affections, but, he reasoned, they are nonetheless always involved in any affective response. According to "the laws of the union which the Creator has fixed between soul and body," they represent the "effects or concomitants" of the soul's affections.[5] In an effort to meet certain problems arising from the revivalism of his time, Edwards attempted to justify a high regard for the affections by associating them with the greater good of the soul. If, he argued, a man's affections arise from and are founded upon the imagination alone—that is, in Reynolds' terms, if they are based solely on the sensitive passions—instead of upon a spiritual enlightenment, then they remain useless and empty.[6] The senses and affections of the body are good when they are subordinate to and employed by the spirit.[7] Because it possesses less life or perfection than the soul, the body should, in accord with the hierarchical scheme evident throughout nature, submit to the soul's instruction. The body is intended by Providence to be the soul's instrument. It follows that since the renewed soul of the saint partially reflects the divine image, his body, as the soul's agent, must in some if less perfect way participate in that image. In fact, considered in relation to the essential harmony between heaven and earth, the body and soul, equally manifestations of these two orders, can be said to share an identical essence: Being, which is the divine love pervading all creation. Through their harmonious and mutual operation, both

---

4. Reynolds, *A Treatise of the Passions*, pp. 37–38.

5. *Religious Affections*, pp. 96–98, 132; and *"The Mind" of Jonathan Edwards*, ed. Leon Howard, p. 108.

6. *Religious Affections*, p. 291.

7. Augustine, *City of God*, 12.5. "The *Body*, though not so noble a part," Willard wrote, "yet is as absolutely necessary to his Being as the Soul" (*A Compleat Body of Divinity*, p. 123; see also p. 126). Reynolds makes the same point (*A Treatise of the Passions*, p. 32).

strive simultaneously toward perfection and goodness in God.[8] Thus the flesh, as the spirit's necessary complement, is a divinely ordained good. Body and soul comprise the whole man.[9]

Adam's whole being evidenced a peaceful harmony and a beautiful order. The appetites and desires of his flesh were appropriately submissive to the dictates of his soul. God did not, according to Reynolds, intend for Adam's senses to possess "*commanding* or moving Power*,*" for they were designed as spiritual agents: "the Action of *Sense* was not from the first Institution ordain'd to touch *Affection*, but to present it selfe primarily to the *Understanding;* upon whose determination and conduct, the Passions were to depend, to submit all their inclinations thereunto, and to be its Ministers."[10] Reynolds is careful to clarify what he means. He is not supporting the sort of rational inhibition or denial of the senses advocated in, say, Plato's *Phaedo;* on the contrary, he is indicating that the body should serve the soul as an instrument and not as a slave.[11] New England Puritan thinkers in the same tradition did not condemn the body's senses or affections, for the flesh remains in every way naturally or inherently good.[12] They were, however, chary of the tendency of the fallen body to be inordinate, to belie its original dignity as the agent of the spirit.

The body was, as the minister of the soul, capable of corruption. At the time of the Fall, Adam's rational soul misled its agent by failing to subordinate it to right reason. Hence Adam shattered the divine image previously reflected by his whole being.

8. Reynolds, *A Treatise of the Passions*, p. 102.

9. "Our nature itself testifies that a man is incomplete unless a body be united with the soul" (Augustine, *City of God*, 10.29). See also David E. Roberts, "The Earliest Writings," in *A Companion to the Study of St. Augustine*, p. 104.

10. Reynolds, *A Treatise of the Passions*, p. 44. See also Augustine, *On Free Choice of the Will*, 1.10.71; 2.18.182. Edwards thought that the "*superior* principles" of the soul were to "maintain an absolute dominion in the heart," whereas the "*inferior* principles" of the natural appetites were "to be wholly subordinate and subservient" (*Original Sin*, pp. 381–82).

11. Reynolds, *A Treatise of the Passions*, pp. 47–48; cf. Plato, *Great Dialogues*, trans. W. H. D. Rouse, pp. 468–70.

12. Reynolds, *A Treatise of the Passions*, pp. 43–44. See also Augustine, *City of God*, 12.3; 14.2.

31

As a result of his disobedience, undisciplined sensory and affective motions rebelled and were transformed into a burden for the sinful soul.[13] To put it another way, the body became a potentially dangerous and mortal instrument. It now seems to enjoy perversity.

In fact, in Adam's descendants the body appears to be in tension with the spirit, just as nature in general seems, as a consequence of the Fall, disjoined from the order of grace. But this conflict is only apparent; it is a manifestation of God's punishment.[14] The flesh in fact remains inherently good: "there is in every Man a native and Originall strugling between *Appetite* and *Reason;* which yet proceedeth from Corruption, and the *Fall* of man, not from *Nature entire:* For, from the law of Creation, there was no formall *Opposition*, but a *Subordination* between *Spirit* and *Sence*."[15] It is owing to the disruption of this psychological hierarchy, to the failure of right reason to direct its less perfect bodily ministers, that the flesh and the spirit take on the appearance of opposing forces.[16]

It is, I think, with this view in mind that we should read most Puritan renunciations of the body. The fallen state of the flesh, not the flesh itself, was spurned by Puritan divines. As a result of its meaning in the English translation of Paul's epistles, the word *flesh* came to refer to the body's fallen state. This meaning is certainly clear in Augustine's discussion of the word,[17] and Jonathan Edwards provides the key to the Puritan understanding of the word in his essay on the Trinity, in which he explains that flesh and spirit are opposed, if by *flesh* is meant sin or corruption and if by *spirit* is intended the opposite of sin.[18] The

13. Augustine, *City of God*, 13.16; 14.3.

14. Ibid., 14.3.

15. Reynolds, *A Treatise of the Passions*, p. 61. Augustine wrote: "the soul is burdened, not by any body whatsoever, but by the body such as it has become in consequence of sin" (*City of God*, 13.16).

16. *City of God*, 13.13.

17. Explaining the ways in which the word *flesh* is used in Scripture, Augustine remarked that insofar as the word means the fallen nature of man himself, it is evil "to live after the flesh . . . though the nature of flesh is not itself evil" (*City of God*, 14.2). Calvin apparently differed in this matter: *Institutes*, 3.3.10.

18. *An Unpublished Essay by Edwards on the Trinity*, ed. George P. Fisher (New York:

term *flesh*, Edwards notes elsewhere, refers to the body's appetites and affections which were once properly subordinated to the spirit but which now are "reigning principles" or "masters of the heart" and thereby—but only thereby—in opposition to the soul.[19] The outcome is an illusive independence and perversity of the body. Man's body, led by the senses instead of by the rational soul, evidences a carnal inclination, a turning away from the concerns of the soul toward matters of the flesh.

ii

These ideas are more often implied than systematically discussed in the writings of Edward Taylor. Although they inform his total vision of man, these concepts tend to contribute less to the specific subject matter of his poems than to the traditional ground upon which they are founded.

Taylor's rejection of a dualism between the temporal and divine orders is relevant to his conception of the body and the soul. For him the fact that men and angels are fellow servants of God is evident in the angelical nature of the human soul (C, p. 302). Indeed, the nature of angels and that of men are so essentially related that "Some are ready to thinke that the Glory of man at the first was Such as did attract the Angells to gaze at him; and the Devells to Envy, and malice him" (C, p. 24).

Adam possessed a body, second in perfection only to that of Christ. In every way his sensory and affective motions were in harmony with the dictates of his rational soul. It was the divine purpose "that all those Glorious Qualifications, and all those admirable Organs of the Bodie of man, so curiously made, and that imortall Soule, that is Seated in the Whole of these, should

---

Scribner's, 1903), p. 98. (Hereafter referred to as *Edwards on the Trinity*.) John Cotton likewise notes that the word *flesh* sometimes refers to the mortal body but generally means "the life of corrupt nature" (*The Way of Life*, p. 283). For Cotton, as for Edwards, the body is, as a body, exempt from blame for sin. Hence, when the conversion process is initiated "the soule begins to loathe it selfe, and to abhor it selfe," not the body (Cotton, p. 5).

19. *Original Sin*, p. 382.

in a most regular way act to the glory of God" (C, p. 314). Adam's "Whole fabrick Consisting of Body and Soule" displayed a beautiful harmony not only between flesh and spirit but also between Adam, the universe, and God.

This harmony was contingent on the body's inherent goodness. As long as it was subordinate to the soul, the body's excellence would manifest itself. Its senses would be like "golden tills" for the two chief faculties of the soul:

> Begracde with Glory, gloried with Grace,
>   In Paradise I was, when all Sweet Shines
> Hung dangling on this Rosy World to face
>   Mine Eyes, and Nose, and Charm mine Eares with Chimes.
>   All these were golden Tills the which did hold
>   My evidences wrapt in glorious folds.
>
>   (1.31, 1–6)

Man's senses, as the windows of the soul (GD, p. 413), originally received divine instruction from nature, instruction which was consistent with right reason and which urged man to respond affectionately to God. Adam, in other words, led a life in which "the Rationall Soule in the body of man, acts the Sensitive body to live a rationall life, by means of its personall Union to it" (C, p. 100).

In spite of his perfection, Adam's "affections were liable to erre in their Naturall motions" (C, p. 445). This does not mean that the capacity for sin lay in the senses or affections of Adam's "Spotless Body" (GD, p. 388). Rather, man's flesh, which possesses less perfection than and exhibits a dependence on the higher goodness of the soul, is unstable without rational guidance. But the body itself, as an aspect of God's phenomenal manifestation, remains free from any natural or inherent tendency to sin, for even "Fallen Nature is not Sinfull Nature before it is Rationall nature" (C, pp. 12–13). Sin is readily manifested in the spirit's bodily agent, but it is solely the product of the rational soul.

The Fall disrupted the initial harmony between the body and the soul. Sin prevented Adam and any of his descendants from benefiting from the divine image once reflected by man's whole being. This loss diminished the excellency of the human body's motions because it impoverished the rational soul by which those motions are animated; both "were Spoiled, and broke to pieces by the Fall" (C, p. 314). Formerly the temple of the Holy Spirit, the whole man, now shattered and threatened by an apparent dualism between the body and the soul, becomes a tenement in ruins. In respect to his body, man finds himself "turnd out of Doors, and so must stay, / Till's house be rais'd against the Reckoning day" (GD, p. 399).

Nowhere, however, does Taylor say that the body is objectively evil. To be sure, he often abjures the flesh, but only insofar as it is a metonymic expression for the overt manifestation of man's fallen condition. In a typically Augustinian passage, Taylor exhorted his parishioners, "so long as the body of sin is in thee, so long thou wilt have the inclination [unto unwarrantable things] vexing of thee" (TCLS, p. 152). This internal commitment to sin—Taylor's use of the word *in* as well as the phrase *body of sin* instead of *sinful body* is significant—adversely affects the body, urging the flesh to war or lust against the spirit. Since the Fall, the misdirected or sin-ridden body appears antagonistic to the soul's endeavors; and it is only in this sense that, in Taylor's view, the flesh has lost its templelike splendor and has degenerated to "Dead Dust" (1.9, 32), a mere "Flesh and Blood bag" (1.30, 27), a "Lump of Slime" (GD, p. 430), and a "Mudwall tent, whose Matters are / Dead Elements, which mixt make dirty trade" (2.75, 13–14). It is only in his unregenerate condition that man bears a "Pallid Pannick Fear upon his Cheeks" (GD, p. 398).

Because the flesh suffers the effects of sin, its motions plague the sinful soul. Its actions appear to turn away from God and seem to prostitute themselves toward carnal ends. Thus Christ admonishes His elect:

> thy senses do inveagle
> Thy Noble Soul to tend the Beagle,
> That t'hunt her games forth go.
>
> (GD, p. 415)

Man's postlapsarian body tends to seek only sensual gratification. "Earth's Toyes" entangle the affections and divert them from their intended purpose (1.24, 29–30). Not only are the best counsels of reason ignored by the flesh, but the understanding, owing to its obscured vision, plays lackey to the "Carnall Whynings" of the senses; reason is "up lockt" in a "Clod of Dust" (GD, p. 430; 1.35, 35).

Despite his frequent reference to the soul's yearning for heavenly joys, Taylor does not contend that the spirit aches for emancipation from the body. The soul's desire for eternal life stems from that inherent inclination toward perfection found throughout creation. It longs for heaven because there it will be restored to its rightful place in the psychological hierarchy, because as long as the senses and affections remain undisciplined and swayed by carnal gratification, the body appears to oppose the greater good of the soul.

While on earth, the saint is engaged in an unrelenting struggle to realign his body and soul. In the postlapsarian world the senses (which inform reason) and the affections (which give vent to the will's motions) often interfere with and even hinder man's search for truth and wisdom. They are now animated by a sin-ridden soul. "Flesh and Blood, are Elementall things" (2.82, 8), and in their unnatural insubordination to the soul they gravitate toward the satisfaction of mere carnal appetites. It is in this sense—and only in this sense—that life can be death, that the human body seems a coffin for the soul ("The Return," ll.39-40). The restoration of the body to its rightful place and dignity as the spirit's agent first requires the rectification of the soul, especially the will. With grace the sinful soul and the fallen body—"Nature's Alembick," with "all its pipes but Sincks of nasty ware" (2.75, 19, 23)—will evince a partially renewed solidarity. Sin, as chapter 3 will argue, is a moral state and thus not inherent in nature or in the flesh. Indeed, what lures man to sin is not his body but his "want of Originall Rightiousness together with a strong inclination unto all actuall evill flowing from the guilt of Adams first Sin over all his posterity."[20]

20. Westfield "Church Record," p. 24.

iii

Taylor considered the Incarnation, albeit at every moment a gracious gift and an unprecedented act, a natural event. I am not suggesting that the Son was in any way coerced by nature to become incarnate, for both his act of creation and his Incarnation were strictly voluntary. I mean that the body, as a part of nature and as a fundamental component of the whole man, consorted from the first with the order of grace and that the Incarnation increases the degree of its participation in the higher realm. Such an interpretation counters the misleading notion, more accurately attributed to such poets as George Herbert and Richard Crashaw, that the Incarnation shocks nature by suddenly yoking it to the transcendent heavenly order. If the two realms are always intertwined, as Taylor's understanding of nature and of the body suggests, then the Incarnation cannot be construed as an *unnatural* occurrence. Indeed, when he wrote "Gods Works done in time are but the Execution of his Eternall Decrees" (C, p. 10), he indicated, as we noted in the last chapter, that earthly or phenomenal time is contingent on and circumscribed by eternity. The awe with which Taylor viewed the Incarnation lay in its redemption of the elect and its more intimate union of nature, especially human nature, with God.

The Son, "Heavens Filler," assumed man's house of clay (2. 24, 42). This assumed human nature, albeit fallen nature (C, pp. 22, 85), was free from fault because flesh is essentially good. Although "it was fallen Nature, and therefore of Sinfull Nature, yet it never was Sinfull Nature" (C, p. 21). Fallen nature, as we noted earlier, "is not Sinfull Nature before it is Rationall nature" (C, pp. 12–13), and Christ's rational nature was, of course, perfect.

The Incarnation, moreover, was a natural event in another sense. It was from the first a part of the Father's creative plan. God, to be sure, did not ordain the commission of sin in order to necessitate Christ's redemptive sacrifice, but his omniscience anticipated man's actions and providentially allowed for sin in the original scheme. The Son in fact consented to his earthly role before God created the world (c, p. 54).[21] Furthermore, although "He was Godhead alone, and without manhood from all Eternity untill his Conception in the Womb" (c, p. 47), the body the Son was to assume existed prior to the creation of the world (c, p. 9).[22] This belief seems less unusual if one recalls that the body per se is incapable of sin, that as a manifestation of nature it participates essentially in the divine order and that it is ultimately slated for perfection.

From this perspective Taylor discerned, as did Milton, a close association between creation and the Incarnation. Just as the Word created and sustains all things—"I Heaven, and Earth do on my shoulders beare," says Christ (GD, p. 392)—so also from the very beginning the Son consented to reassert and give impetus to his creation through the Incarnation. The Incarnation accomplished this in two ways: it reinstated a few chosen individuals into the plan of creation and it effected a more perfect mingling of the earthly and heavenly orders. That the Incarnation reasserted creation is clear in Taylor's depiction of the two events in terms of the hierarchical degrees of glory:

> In Mans Creation Something of Gods Graciousness did shine out on man, in that Glorie and State that he was advanced unto. But it was little comparatively, and as for mercy perhaps none, that did shine forth. But in that as greate a glory, if not in Some Sense a greater, of the Godhead was lying in them, as in any other Divine properties, God did for the Shining forth of their glorious beams permit the darkness of Sin to invade mankinde . . . and all Gods transactings with fallen man in order to his recovery, are discoveries of the Glorie of Gods Grace, and Mercy. But the greatest discovery of this glory as the Essentiall Root lump of these Glorious

---

21. For similar views of the Father's covenant with the Son before creation, see Increase Mather, *The Mystery of Christ*, p. 6, and Edwards, *Freedom of the Will*, p. 286.
22. See also Augustine, *The Trinity*, 1.7.14.

beams, ariseth from this Personall Union of our Nature to the
Divine Nature in the Lord Christ.

(C, p. 91)

Since Taylor thought of the Incarnation as a promotion of the
entire creation to a further display of glory, it is not surprising
that he portrayed this second act as a renewal, a renovation, and
a new creation, culminating in "new Heavens, and new earth"
(C, pp. 64, 96, 126).

The work of both the creation and the Incarnation lay in the
auspices of the Son: "as the Works of Creation, and Providence
. . . be the works of Christ: So also the Worke of Regeneration"
(C, p. 55). Taylor depicted creation and its maintenance, as we
observed in chapter 1, in reference to the hands of the Son. Its
reassertion or re-creation likewise fell (Taylor's pun) into his
hands (1.31, 32). Christ's regenerating hands extend this new
creation especially to man. Although Adam sundered his original relationship as an adopted son of God and as a "brother" of
the Son, his saintly successors are "born again" and "made new
Creatures" through Christ's reassertion of creation (C, pp. 321,
221).

The most vital aspect of his reassertion of creation is Christ's
real and inseparable union of God and man. Although heaven
and earth always share an essential tie, Christ's hypostatic (C, p.
29) or *theanthropic* (2.44, 10; C, p. 4) union of the divine and
human natures engenders a personal affiliation. It emphasizes,
on the one hand, the place of nature in God's plan (grace is
conveyed by natural means): "Christ, in His treating men, is
pleased to treat them as men, else He would never have taken
man's nature upon Him" (TCLS, p. 17). It provides, on the other
hand, a closer, richer, more vital relation to God: this union "is
the greatest Mystery in all the Creation of God. It is the Wonder-
fullst advancement given to our Nature that created nature is,
or Can be capable of; it lifts it up almost into Deity itselfe" (C,
p. 103).

This advancement results from Christ's assumption of the
whole being of man. His rational soul consists, like that of every

man, of reason and will. His reason is, however, free from any enfeeblement of the "Visive Spirits" and retains "no mote to marre" its sight; his will acts according to the "Cleare light" of the understanding and can not "be Stalld by the least inclination to resist" (C, p. 177). Furthermore, Christ's perfect bodily senses and affections are subordinate to this soul. They are so harmonious in their motions that they never evidence "the least jar in them to attend the Dictates of reason." With the exception of the moral condition of Original Sin, Christ assumed human nature in its physical and spiritual fullness.

Because Christ became true man, the whole being of the saint is renewed by divine grace (TCLS, p. 23). This means, among other things, that the dignity of the saint's body is reaffirmed. The Incarnation rejuvenates and elevates the essential tie between the flesh and the spirit. Although after the Fall man's being is a mere "Mortall Chip," it never loses, despite the effects of sin, its fundamental connection to God, the "Eternall Plank" (2.18, 21–22). When Christ, the "Eternall Plank" or the tree of life, reasserted this essential relation and joined immortal Godhead and mortal manhood, human nature—the body and soul, the whole man—was reconverted into "Choice Timber Rich" (2.29, 19).

The saints are the branches of this fruit-bearing tree. They are specially elected (though only God knows why) and, like timber, are destined to serve a purpose: the glorification of God. Their souls have been rescued by Christ from eternal damnation and their entire being has been freshly retimbered by grace. The elect now share in a new affiliation with God: "there is not onely a Mysticall Relation between Christ, and his Church but also a Naturall, by this personall Union. . . . We are members of his Body, of his Flesh, and of his Bones" (C, p. 85). Man's nature "as we are man Kinde," Taylor explained, is less perfect than but identical to that of Christ: "And so he, and wee are united together (*Genere*) in one and the Same common Nature. This indeed gives the Pagan as reall propriety in Christ, and as true a Claim to him as to the true Believer" (C, p. 320). As these passages and so many other similar ones throughout Taylor's writings make clear, the human body is ennobled and glorified by the Incarnation.

For the elect this personal union in Christ provides the basis for the regenerative process. Taylor would have agreed with Willard's explanation that this process signified a union of the saint's whole being with Christ, a union which is "not meerly and purely relative; it is a real thing."[23] The regenerative process concerns the body as well as the soul:

> Thou now didst sweep Death's Cave
> Clean with thy hand: and leavest not a dust
> Of Flesh, or Bone that there th'Elect dropt have,
> But bringst out all, new buildst the Fabrick just,
> (Having the Scrowle of Gods Displeasure clear'd)
> Bringst back the Soule putst in its tent new rear'd.
>
> (2.95, 25–30)

The saint's body, though it never underwent any radical loss of goodness, is the "tent new rear'd"; it is the refabricated tabernacle (*tabernaculum* is the Latin word for *tent*) designed to house the soul which, in turn, is clothed in the new fabric of grace, Christ's wedding garment, an image discussed in the following chapter. Christ's marriage or election of a saint makes his whole being heaven-bound; in heaven the inherent goodness of both the body and the soul will shine forth. No longer will the affections "range / As yelping beagles doe" (GD, p. 416), for the body will be perfected, like Christ's flesh, from "a piece of China Clay / Formd up into a China Dish" (2.143, 13–14). As these images imply, the body's essence remains unchanged. Clay remains essentially clay; it will merely reflect a further manifestation of the artistry of Christ's creative hands.

Grace, therefore, influences the affections of the body. Taylor emphasized the affections, especially love, because as mental and physical expressions of the soul they are an index to a man's moral state. Although he certainly realized that no single, satisfactory means existed to determine his moral condition with

23. Willard, *A Compleat Body of Divinity*, p. 430; also p. 455.

certitude and although he humbly resigned himself to God's mysterious will, Taylor looked to his affective responses for an indication of his standing with God. To possess only "Frozen Affection," to bear only "Icikles of Frostbitt Love" probably evidenced an unregenerate, "Congealed Heart" (1.14, 37–40). "Right mannaged affections," on the other hand, particularly the love of God, most likely testified to the salutary effect of grace (C, p. 128). Again and again Taylor renounced his dull, "Chilly Numbd Affections" and asked Christ to melt them with his Love's grace so that they would flowerlike "up their heads in Love flames reare" (1.14, 45–46; 2.121, 3–4).

It is apparent, therefore, that certain aspects of Taylor's view of the Incarnation and of the outcome of the regenerative process reveal his high regard for the nature of the human body. The flesh, when properly guided under the tutelage of the regenerated rational soul, can demonstrate, while on earth, some degree of its God-given dignity. In fact, when his senses serve an enlightened reason and when his affections respond to a loving will, a man may legitimately entertain thoughts of his salvation. It is this idea—the need to reestablish the soul's supremacy and thereby to reassert the essential goodness of the body—which underlies Taylor's complaints against the flesh. He did not consider the body to be innately depraved but believed that in its fallen state it needed to be realigned with the soul, to be put in accord with the original hierarchical scheme Providence had designed for it: "The Richest Jewell in the Cabinet / Of Nature made, this Spirituall Life is set" (2.89, 47–48). This is what Taylor meant when he advised each man to strive to "lift" himself "out against the flesh under the conduct of the Spirit" (TCLS, p. 193). The saint is not to desire to be separated or released from his body but is to exercise his soul in such a fashion as to redeem the flesh, to manage his soul in such a manner as to direct both it and the body to eternal life.[24] Just as the corruptions of the body are the result of the sin of the soul, so it must

24. "Knowing that the cause of this burdensomeness is not the nature and substance of the body, but its corruption, we do not desire to be deprived of the body, but to be clothed with its immortality" (Augustine, *City of God*, 14.3).

be the revived soul which sets about the task of redeeming the flesh—the two are inseparable. If one can achieve some semblance of this initial order and harmony between the flesh and the spirit, then he may well be a child of God.

iv

In order to reinforce the argument that creation and the Incarnation declare the goodness and the necessity of the flesh in God's design, a few words should be said regarding the place of the human body after the Second Advent. First, there exists the matter of Christ's body, a concern which proved a thorny problem for many of the church fathers. Taylor specifically refuted Calvin's teaching that Christ resides in heaven solely in his deity, that in some manner he converted or subsumed his manhood into his Godhead. Commenting on the shortsightedness of this idea, Taylor remarks, "why the Humanity of the person in personall Union to the Godhead should be deprived of it, in which the Mediatory Offices were carried on, I see no proof nor reason" (c, pp. 412–13). In order for Christ to remain the eternal mediator between God and man, Taylor reasoned, he must dwell in heaven with his Godhead and manhood eternally joined in a personal union (c, p. 50).

It is true that although it shares in divine Being, created nature cannot be deified; for created nature had a beginning and must be sustained by God, both of which mean that it can never become one with God. Through Christ, however, human nature is advanced as close to deity as created nature can be (c, pp. 25, 92, 416). The Incarnation, in fact, elevates man beyond the angels. Hence in "The Experience" Taylor, in the persona of an elect everyman, tells the angels to move aside and somewhat acrimoniously berates them—doubtless owing to a hyperbolic figurative context and to an overexuberance on the poet's part—for standing further from the Godhead than he; "My Nature is your Lord," he punned, "and doth Unite / Better than Yours unto the Deity" (19–22).[25]

25. See also 1.8, 29; 1.9, 26–27; 2.44, 36–42. Mather apparently did not agree with

Similarly, nature in general benefits, for the "Carnall String" of the Incarnation "Did raise Earths Tunes above the Heavenly Quire" (2.120, 15–16). But it is human nature in which Taylor was most interested. Not only is it elevated above the angels, but it is also contained in the Trinity. This idea, possibly learned from Augustine, represents a logical extension of Taylor's belief that Christ's body existed before creation and that in his eternal mediatory capacity he still retains his manhood.[26] Because human nature was fused with divine nature through Christ's personal union, Taylor concluded, the "being and Essence" of created nature now exist "in the midst of the Trinity" (C, p. 92).

The Incarnation also affected the destiny of the whole being of the saint. At the time of the Second Advent his body will be resurrected, immortalized, and reunited to the soul.[27] What man receives at the final judgment is not a new but a renewed body. Men will receive "the very same parts of the Same bodies" which they possessed on earth (C, p. 221).[28] To be sure, these bodies will be made over, as if through a new creation. But they will be composed "of their own Materialls, their own dust"; they will possess the flesh and bones of their former existence (C, p. 62).

No Puritan was comfortable predicting what powers this restored, immortal body would enjoy. Nevertheless, in spite of their wariness to detail the heavenly joys—conversely, many were quite specific about the punishments of hell—Puritan divines were inclined to assume that since the saint's body was

---

this unusual, if figurative, view; he held that although man was below the angels in his first estate, he had been made *equal* to them since the Incarnation (*The Mystery of Christ*, p. 155).

26. See Augustine, *The Trinity*, 14.18.24.

27. According to Augustine there are two chief stages in the regenerative process. The first is the spiritual rebirth of the saint resulting from the gift of faith. The second is the rebirth of the body at the final judgment (*City of God*, 13.17; 20.6).

28. Taylor noted in the Westfield "Church Record": "the very same body that Died shall rise again, & not a new one made, but it onely made anew. . . . And the very same Soule that Departed & not an other shall enter into the very same Body out of which it departed" (p. 63). See also C, pp. 62–63, 83; Augustine, *City of God*, 10.30; Westminster Confession, 32.2; and Reynolds, *A Treatise of the Passions*, p. 424.

entire and since its responses originate in the rational soul, then doubtless the resurrected body experienced some sort of affections. One could, they argued, appropriately compare the delights of heaven to the pleasures derived from the rationally governed senses of the earthly body.[29] Edwards went beyond a mere comparison. He held that in heaven the elect would experience certain physical pleasures of the temporal world. At least in the matter of love and joy, he explained, the heavenly experience of affections is of the same nature as that of man's earthly experience, though the degree and circumstances of the former are superior.[30]

To be sure, this body would undergo a transformation in its heavenly state. Puritans had learned from Paul that the natural body was destined to be converted into a spiritual body (1. Cor. 15: 44). Augustine, commenting on Paul's meaning, wrote that the body will not be changed into spirit but will be made spiritual. It will still be flesh, but it would be completely subservient to the spirit. To Augustine this perfect obedience constituted the spiritualization of the flesh.[31]

Though Taylor is not specific about the nature of heavenly joy, his poems suggest that heavenly affections, albeit more perfect, are not unlike those of the temporal life. In "The Experience," for instance, he explains that if he were elected by Christ, heaven would seem less to him after his death because he will have experienced on earth so much of the affections to be enjoyed in that glorious realm. In Taylor's view the body's form will be transformed in such a manner that it will, as we noted, be somewhat like Christ's body; it will enjoy what Christ's body finds pleasurable (2.76, 25–26). The body of the saint will possess the same soul it had on earth (c, pp. 221–22) and will in no way interfere with the operation of the spirit. The flesh will be spiritualized in the sense that it will, through perfect obedience, com-

---

29. Richard Baxter, *The Saints Everlasting Rest*, p. 322. The case for Baxter's influence on Puritan meditative tradition has been made by Louis L. Martz, *The Poetry of Meditation: A Study of English Religious Literature of the Seventeenth Century*, rev. ed., pp. 153–75.

30. Edwards, *Religious Affections*, p. 113.

31. Augustine, *City of God*, 13.20,24; 22.21.

plement the soul. Together they will harmoniously function for the glory of God. Taylor thus wrote of the church militant and, by implication, of the elect dwelling in heaven:

> Thy Intellects a Saphrin Socket bears
>   Christ's flaming Torch of Grace that sanctifies.
> Thy Will Christ's Cabinet of Rich Grace Wares
>   Top full of Grace of Every Sort and Sise.
> Thy Body's like a golden Lanthorn trim
>   Through which the lamps of Grace shine from within.
>   (2.135, 7–12)

It is appropriate that in a poem entitled "A Fig for thee Oh! Death," Taylor used erotic images derived from the flesh in order to suggest the intimacy and reality of this future harmony between the body and the soul: "The Soule and Body now, as two true Lovers / Ery night how do they hug and kiss each other" (47–48).

v

In the light of these comments it is, I think, erroneous to interpret Taylor's conception of the human body from a Platonic point of view. Though he certainly lamented the corrupt state of the flesh, he did not see the body as the prison of a soul yearning for release. It is somewhat misleading to conclude about Taylor that by "spreading out his devotion, by giving it a wider base in his entire life, by denying as strenuously as he could in his whole behavior the duality of body and spirit, and by making himself personally and socially, in his family, church, and community, the whole creation of God, he somewhat relieved the tension that nearly undid John Donne."[32] In Taylor's works, as in those of

32. Grabo, *Edward Taylor*, p. 8. It is surprising that Grabo takes this position, for later he notes both that Taylor believes man's nature to be seated in the Trinity and that "the world of the *Meditations* storms constantly with an impressive variety of shapes, colors, odors, and feelings" (pp. 17–18, 158). It is equally surprising that he should conclude that Taylor's poetic perspective is "unnatural" because the poet makes "earth and heaven impinge one upon another" (p. 159); this very observation pinpoints the limita-

Donne, there exists no real or objective conflict between the natural and heavenly orders. Taylor emphasized the whole man. This is why he abjured a mere mental or contemplative response to God, why he looked even beyond his *Preparatory Meditations* and to his affections for a sign of the effects of converting grace on his entire being: "Oh! that I ever felt what I profess" (1.35, 1). In spite of the fact that he deplored the rebellious state of fallen flesh and that he thought Original Sin was transmitted through "Spermatick Principalls," Taylor did not advocate the stoical suppression of the senses and affections. Human nature becomes sinful nature only when it becomes rational nature; though it manifests itself through the soul's bodily agent, sin nevertheless lies solely in the rational soul.

With this perspective it is not difficult to reconcile Taylor's tirades against the flesh. By the word *flesh* he meant the body's moral or subjective condition resulting from sin. This word, as Paul used it and as Edwards explained it in his essay of the Trinity, became a shorthand expression signifying the corrupted state of the body. That is to say, it meant the postlapsarian condition in which the body, bereft of proper guidance, appears to be in tension with the soul. Taylor, as did other Puritan ministers, spoke harshly of the flesh, in this sense, in order to convey to his parishioners the necessity of renouncing the present carnal emphasis of their bodies; then they might strive for a more proper alignment between the body and the soul. They were to seek for the subordination of the flesh "under the conduct of the Spirit." And when, upon occasion, Taylor berated the body in his meditations, he

---

tions of Grabo's Platonic or mystical reading of Taylor's verse. For Taylor the union of heaven and earth is, as I have argued, like that of the body and soul—a most *natural* conjunction, free from any inherent tension or conflict. Kenneth B. Murdock also perceives too distinct a line between Taylor's conception of the human senses and of the soul (*Literature and Theology in Colonial New England*, p. 157). The tension between heaven and earth which these critics discern is of a different order, as E. F. Carlisle suggests: "even though Christ reconciles the great disparity between God and man, the gap or abyss paradoxically remains because God is still agent and man recipient" ("The Puritan Structure of Edward Taylor's Poetry," *American Quarterly*, 20, Summer 1968, 151).

did so for the same reason; he employed the poetic device of meiosis[33] in order to impress upon himself an image not of the inherent evil of the body but rather of its corrupted moral condition. The only real resolution of the apparent conflict between the spirit and the flesh resulting from the postlapsarian moral state of the soul lies in grace, which reinvigorates the soul and reinstates the defiled body to its rightful place:

> Oh! make my Body, Lord, Although its vile,
> Thy Warehouse where Grace doth her treasures lay.
> And Cleanse the house and ery Room from Soile.
> Deck all my Rooms with thy rich Grace I pray.
>
> (2.75, 55–58)

If the soul, a "Bird of Paradise," has indeed been "put in / This Wicker Cage (my Corps) to tweedle praise," then each man is to "live up unto God's Word in soul and body" (TCLS, p. 189). As divergent as significant aspects of their theology are, Taylor would doubtless have wholeheartedly agreed with John Donne's conviction—also found in the works of John Milton—that God intends for man to strive continually for a harmonious integration of body and soul and to direct, by means of this effort, his whole being to God: "they [body and soul] must serve God joyntly together, because God having joyned them, man may not separate them, but as God shall re-unite them at the last Resurrection, so must we, in our own Resurrections in this life."[34]

---

33. Charles W. Mignon discusses Taylor's use of this device in "Edward Taylor's *Preparatory Meditations*: A Decorum of Imperfection," *PMLA*, 83 (October 1968), 1423–28.
34. Donne, *Sermons*, ed. George Potter and Evelyn Simpson, 7: 107–8.

CHAPTER III

A Viper's Nest,
the Featherbed of Faith

THE WILL

Although Edward Taylor considered reason as the first faculty of the rational soul to be affected by grace, his poetry reveals that the will or heart—he used the terms interchangeably[1]—received the focus of his attention. In fact, if one predominant subject recurs throughout the *Preparatory Meditations* and *Gods Determinations*, it is the centrality of the will and its principal affection of love in the drama of a saint's conversion. This emphasis can be found again and again in the numerous diaries, journals, meditations, biographies, and sermons of early New England. Such writings clearly indicate that the will or heart was consciously and unconsciously of foremost importance in Puritan thought.[2]

---

1. "By the *heart* you must not understand, that fleshly part of the body which is the seate of life. . . . But it is meant the *will* of a man, which lyes in the heart, for as the *understanding* lyes in the *head* or braine, so the *will* is seated in the *heart*" (Cotton, *The Way of Life*, p. 127).

2. Although Cynthia G. Wolff rightly notes that concern with the will pervaded Puritan culture, she stresses only the deleterious effects of this preoccupation ("Literary Reflections of the Puritan Character," *Journal of the History of Ideas*, 29, January-March 1968, 13–32).

Puritan regard for the will was largely inherited from Augustine and Calvin. Augustine not only referred throughout his works to the role of this faculty in man, indeed to its ultimate primacy over intellect, but more significantly placed it at the vital core of Christian psychology. From Augustinian tradition Puritans learned to think of the will as a positive, integrating power. They were, of course, influenced by Calvin's teachings which, despite their relation to Augustinian thought, tended to reflect the negative, disruptive nature of the fallen and depraved condition of the will. Calvin's concern with this faculty led him to conclude not only that God's main attribute is his arbitrary will but also that the will of fallen man exercises so much power that it continually dwarfs the function of reason in the experience of regeneration.[3] Besides this theological heritage, the experience of Puritans in the New World doubtless reinforced their focus on the will. They envisioned that God had called them to employ their collective will in founding his City on the Hill, and in the New World they encountered a land the physical features of which demanded a strong sense of will from its settlers. Early Puritan society was determined, almost as if it were reasserting the act of genesis, to exercise its collective will and to carve out of the American wilderness a physically and morally ordered community of God.

In order to define the motivation behind and the distinctive nature of Edward Taylor's verse, it is necessary to recognize the importance of the will in his thought. His theory of language and specifically his notions of meditative poetry—the subjects of the next two chapters—are founded on his psychological and theological interpretation of the will. This chapter considers the major particulars of his view of this faculty. First, Taylor endorsed the Augustinian notion of the will as an integrating power, one which joins the understanding and the affections as well as unites

---

3. Calvin, *Institutes*, 2.2. Calvin, of course, never completely dismissed the value of reason; see William C. dePauley, *The Candle of the Lord: Studies in the Cambridge Platonists*, pp. 231–44.

man's body and soul. Second, he believed that in this faculty lay the origin of sin; for Taylor evil is rooted in the depraved mental disposition of a perverse will, and, it follows, this faculty must become the final locus of Christ's grace in the experience of conversion. Third, Taylor reflected the Christian tradition which associates this faculty with the Holy Spirit, an idea informing the poet's concern with love as the most vital of the heart's affections. Finally, his reflection of the Puritan interpretation of practical piety is related to the preeminence of the will in his thought.

i

Although in Puritan theology God's natural image tends to be identified with the human understanding, this association actually includes the will; for the divine image was believed to be reflected by the whole soul of man, reason and will. Moreover, since these two faculties of the rational soul depend on the body's senses for information and express themselves through affective motions, God's image must be impressed not merely on the rational soul but on man's entire being. However, of these components of the whole man, the will plays the pivotal role. The soul's eye, according to the tenets of faculty psychology, perceives truth and wisdom through the senses and conveys its judgments to the will; the will in turn moves the affections and thereby manifests its decision to accept or reject the dictates of the understanding. Since the understanding, when functioning properly, discerns the truth in the revealed will of God as expressed in Scripture and in nature—natural law and the law of reason are one—and since this divine wisdom determines the motions of the human will, the heart is obliged, in accord with the natural hierarchy God has built into the soul, to be guided by and to obey reason's findings.[4] Consequently, if the understanding evidences a "spirituall deadness," the will remains incapacitated and unable to

4. See Augustine, *The Trinity*, 10.11.17, 15.27.50; Milton, *Paradise Lost*, 9: 351–56; Baxter, *The Saints Everlasting Rest*, p. 281; Willard, *A Compleat Body of Divinity*, p. 460; and Edwards, *Freedom of the Will*, p. 370.

operate rightly (2.131, 11–12); for the will depends on a preceding enlightenment of the soul's eye by God's grace for its own spiritual motivation (1.16, 5–10, GD, p. 407). Left to itself, the will flails about aimlessly in the dark; but guided by an illuminated intellect, the heart discovers in right actions what the informing faculty has perceived as truth. Many Puritan thinkers held, therefore, that though it shares the throne of the rational soul with the understanding, the will should exemplify a subservience to the more regal faculty. In fact, though the will can refuse to listen to or act in harmony with the dictates of reason, it can never sway the hierarchically superior faculty to assent to anything contrary to the wisdom it has discerned.[5]

In God's original design for them, of course, these two powers were not intended to conflict with one another. The will, though it possessed a certain liberty and independence from reason, was from the first inclined to conform to the motions of the intellectual faculty.[6] Just as reason naturally leans toward truth, the healthy will chooses good and, with the wisdom of reason, greatest good or God. The mutual end of the rational soul's two faculties was intended by their Creator to be achieved through their harmonious interaction in the search for truth and goodness. Reason, as the eye of the soul and the proper seat of knowledge, should, by means of the will, facilitate the way in which the light of wisdom "dasheth all its powerfull beaming Influences over the whole man"; for it is the will or heart, as the center of man's entire being, which finally becomes "the house into which this Sun shines" (C, p. 371). Again and again Taylor's poetry depicts this sequential relation between reason and will: "fill my Spirits Eye with light to see. / Make in my heart thy Kingly Sunshine flame" (2.54, 46–47); "Lord feed mine eyes then with thy Doings rare, / And fat my heart with these ripe fruites thou bearst" (2.56, 55–56);

---

5. Reynolds, *A Treatise of the Passions*, p. 541.

6. See Edwards, *Religious Affections*, p. 96; Perry Miller, "Jonathan Edwards on the Sense of the Heart," *Harvard Theological Review*, 41 (April 1948), 136.

> Oh! that I had but halfe an eye to view
> This excellence of thine, undazled: so
> Therewith to give my heart a touch anew
> Untill I quickned am, and made to glow.
>
> (2.1, 25–28)

Since the thoughtful judgments of the understanding always inform the will (2.91, 13), it is not surprising that Taylor expressed a heartfelt discontent whenever he rationally meditated on life in heaven and on his own unworthiness: "This thought on, sets my heart upon the Rack" (2.82, 5). In order to ease his remorse, he urged his intellectual faculty to perceive God's "Argument," the pointed truth of which might medicinally lance his heart (1.36, 71–72). In other words, he sought the illumination of reason in order that his will would likewise be renewed (2.119, 26–28), for only when the intellect first bears the light of "Christ's flaming Torch of Grace that sanctifies" can the will be converted into grace's faithful storehouse, a "Cabinet of Rich Grace Wares / Top full of Grace of Every Sort and Sise" (2.135, 8–10). In short, Taylor sought that unity of the rational soul's faculties, whereby, as exemplified in unfallen Adam and most perfectly embodied in Christ (C, p. 177), the heart functions harmoniously within its proper hierarchical relation to reason.

It is evident from the foregoing comments that for Taylor these two powers, though intimately related, are somewhat distinct.[7] Whether by choice or perhaps owing to the fragmentation attending analytical discourse, many early Puritan thinkers differentiated between reason and will. Doubtless they were indirectly influenced by the classical tradition which maintained that there was a decided difference between the morality founded on the will and that rooted in reason, with the latter far superior to the former.[8] Nevertheless, the heart was said to be engaged in some way with every action of the understanding. In fact, Augustine had argued that reason is unable to perceive

7. Grabo offers another view: that Taylor "thinks of the will as a tendency of the whole understanding, and as an inclination rather than a faculty" (TCLS, p. xli).

8. See Charles N. Cochrane, *Christianity and Classical Culture: A Study of Thought and Action from Augustus to Augustine*, pp. 507–8.

truth without involving the will.[9] In other words, these two powers may possess separate identities, but they are unable to act separately. This point, a subtle distinction often obscured or nearly lost in Puritan discussions of these powers, implies neither that the will can bind the understanding nor that reason can force the will, which always remains "the Mistresse of her own Operation";[10] what is meant is that they comprise the entire rational soul and that every motion of the soul inescapably involves both of them. What the reason knows is inseparably joined to what the will loves.

There exists, moreover, a simultaneity in the operation of reason and will, a point too often omitted in Puritan discussions of the hierarchical relationship of the faculties. The sequence from reason to will is not measurable in terms of time. This view of their concurrent action underlies Taylor's observation that "all things come to urge us to an Universall Conformity to his Doctrine and Laws: this will be our Wisdom" (C, p. 136). Taylor's comment, echoing Augustine's belief that everything naturally turns with love toward perfect Being, indicates that the proper exercise of the will, the faculty with which one conforms, fulfills the quest of reason for wisdom. Put another way, what satisfies one faculty necessarily pleases the other; a mutual state of being, "an Universall Conformity" in a more narrow sense, is achievable only when they both agree on the same object for their concerted motion.

Concerning the relation of the will to the affections, early New England Puritan thought is fairly consistent. Affective motions were understood to be inseparable from the will. They were, as we noted in chapter 2, designed to remain subordinate to, de-

9. *On Free Choice of the Will*, 3.24.254. Edwards developed the idea by arguing that there cannot "be a clear distinction made between the two faculties of understanding and will, as acting distinctly and separately.... When the mind is sensible of the sweet beauty and amiableness of a thing, that implies a sensibleness of sweetness and delight in the presence of the idea of it: and this sensibleness of the amiableness or delightfulness of beauty, carries in the very nature of it, the sense of the heart; or an effect and impression the soul is the subject of, as a substance possessed of taste, inclination and will" (*Religious Affections*, p. 272). See also Reynolds, *A Treatise of the Passions*, p. 61 and Rosemond Tuve, *Elizabethan and Metaphysical Imagery*, p. 397.

10. Reynolds, *A Treatise of the Passions*, p. 518.

pendent upon, and totally obedient to the will (C, p. 209). Certain divines argued that the affections are in some sense autonomous and that their subordination to the will is voluntary, but more commonly early Puritans thought of them as modes of the will's expression.[11] Taylor saw them as essentially related to the inclination of the entire soul, in particular to that of the will. For Taylor every act of the will engendered an affective response.[12] Hence, whenever Taylor requested God to fill his "Hide bound Heart. Harder than mountain Rocks," with grace, he also had in mind the condition of his affections, the frozen or thawed state of which depended on the moral stance of his will (2.118, 1–5). It is natural, then, that speaking as Adam in "The Ebb and Flow" Taylor should write, "My heart was made thy tinder box. / My 'ffections were thy tinder in't" (2–3). Taylor was seeking grace's restoration of his will and its affections. The affections are "the feet of the soul, the handmaids of the will";[13] as such they are inseparable from the motions of the whole soul.

Equally evident in this scheme of the faculties is the Augustinian view of the will as an intermediate good,[14] in which capacity the heart unites the body and the soul. As Taylor explained in "A Particular Church is God's House," it is "the Uniting Faculty."[15] This idea deserves careful attention in a discussion of the function of the will in Puritan theological and psychological thought, especially as expressed in Taylor's poetry. Although, as we shall shortly see, he recognized it as the seat of sin and the source of the apparent disruption of God's order, Taylor did not construe the will as a demonic faculty, the depravity of which overpowers a man and reduces him to a state

11. In commenting on this controversy Willard refused to inquire whether the affections are a distinct faculty but concluded that there exists "a concomitancy of them in the act of believing" (p. 454). Miller discusses the affections in *The New England Mind*, 1: 252–54.

12. See also Reynolds, *A Treatise of the Passions*, p. 48; Edwards, *Religious Affections*, pp. 96–97 and *Freedom of the Will*, pp. 309–10.

13. Willard, *A Compleat Body of Divinity*, p. 211.

14. Augustine, *On Free Choice of the Will*, 2.19.196.

15. MS, Boston Public Library, p. 36.

of helpless servitude to its destructive whims. On the contrary, Taylor derived from the notion of its integrating function the idea that the will is the pivotal animating mechanism of the whole man, that it represents the core of an individual's self, the entirety of his being. Taylor thus focused on the heart as a synecdoche for the whole man, as the key faculty to be considered in the determination of his spiritual condition—an observation to bear in mind when considering his emphasis on "heart examination" in his "Spiritual Relation."[16] This focus was partly attributable to his belief that, although the faith accompanying God's saving grace first influences reason, it must finally reside in the will. Rooted in the heart, grace and faith begin the reunification of the whole man; they initiate the process whereby the harmonious, loving interpenetration of reason and will as well as of the rational soul and its bodily instrument will be restored.

A purified heart betokens a purified man, for each person *is* his will.[17] Mediating between the soul and the body, this faculty signifies the "Whole man" or self, which "will be full of Light" when the heart yields to God's grace (C, p. 397). It is through his will that a man must "Labour to bring both the inward and outward man into a Conformity unto Christs Doctrine, and Rules" (C, p. 135). The more harmonious is the interaction between one's body and soul, it follows, the more likely is one's will experiencing the regenerative process.

ii

Although it always operates in conjunction with reason and the

16. Stanford, "Edward Taylor's 'Spiritual Relation,' " *American Literature*, 35 (January 1964), 472.

17. Referring to the will as "that part that was most *vitall*," as "the chiefest part of the soule," Cotton concludes that "As the mans heart is, so is the man" (*The Way of Life*, pp. 128, 133, 220). He further remarks "the great command, which the heart hath over the whole man," emphasizing that "according to the temper of the heart, such is the temper of the whole man; if the heart be good, though the affections should be disordered, and the eyes wanton, if the will be right, all is right"; for "upon whatsoever the heart is set, to that the eye looks, and the ear attends, every thing acts towards it, all goes freely that way, the mind, the judgement, the invention, the affection, and what ever a man hath, it all works that way" (pp. 205–6).

affections, the will alone possesses the power of choice.[18] The freedom of this faculty is, however, limited by natural law, by which is meant that tendency of everything to lean toward the greatest good, toward loving conformity with the will of God. As the first cause and the ultimate end of all things, "God, and His All, 's the Object of the Will: / All God alone can onely it up fill" (GD, p. 440).[19]

In spite of its inherent desire to love God and the fact that its every motion is circumscribed by the divine will, the heart is never coerced to obey God. Even in Adam it was free to continue in obedience to its radical inclination or, in conjunction with the misapprehension of reason, to turn away from greatest good and pridefully enjoy itself.[20] That God foreknew Adam's Fall in no way reduced this freedom. Everything Adam did was voluntary, for "according to the law of Nature it is most certain, that every particular agent is the proper Author of its own Act, Whether the Act is Regular or Irregular"; by "regular" Taylor means those actions of "Subordinate Agents" which conform to the goodness inherent in "the Law of their Natures as Created." Though all actions inevitably serve God's ends, sinful behavior must be attributed to the individual will and is "not at all to be appropriated to Providence" (C, p. 117). Other than the will nothing else in nature can resist its natural inclination toward the goodness of the divine will. Since it manifests this power of choice, the will is centrally significant in regard to Taylor's view of (a) the nature of sin and (b) the experience of conversion.

(a) Taylor did not think of sin in Manichean terms. He never

18. The "heart or will of a man, is that whereby we chuse or refuse a thing" (Cotton, *The Way of Life*, p. 127).

19. See also Augustine, *City of God*, 14.13. Edwards wrote that "we mean nothing else, by Greatest Good, but that which agrees most with the inclination and disposition of the soul" ("*The Mind*," p. 85); also Edwards, *Religious Affections*, p. 255.

20. See Basil Willey, *The Seventeenth Century Background*, p. 14 and Westminster Confession, 4.2; 9.1. Milton wrote: "God left free the Will, for what obeyes / Reason, is free, and Reason he made right" (*Paradise Lost*, 9:351–52). John Donne explains the relation of this freedom to God's will in a sermon in which he argues that "to assent or dis-assent is our own; we may choose which we will doe . . . ; But though this faculty be ours, it is ours, but because God hath imprinted it in us. So that still to will, as well as to doe, to beleeve, as well as to work, is all from God" (*Sermons*, 10:89).

attributed to God the creation of evil as a force opposed to good. He maintained neither that the flesh was created with sinful tendencies nor that angelic or human wills possessed the seed of rebellion. Contrary to Calvin, Taylor did not assert that Adam fell as a result of a natural defect in his will.[21] The will, though certainly able to commit sin, was created good and predisposed toward good, a notion fully exonerating God from any complicity in Adam's Fall. In no manner can God be blamed for sin because his Being is totally righteous and because every aspect of creation is continually generated by his love and thereby partakes of his Being. Indeed, sin is evil in that it opposes this Being and love. Thus "Sin can no way bee reflected upon God, as its Authour," for "God never gave, by either the Law of Nature, or of Divine Institution, any authority to anyone to do what in its own nature is Evill" (C, pp. 117, 403).

Before his Fall the innate motivation of Adam's will and the desires of his body were not in tension (1.31, 1–6). So long as his will relied on reason's instruction Adam experienced a harmonious union between his body and his soul. Together reason and will directed Adam's whole being toward the attainment of greatest good. While his will remained thus inclined, it maintained its freedom. If Adam displayed any pride, it was reflected in his humble recognition that his life was dependent upon and related to God, whose "Being Being gave to all that be." It follows that since the Fall resulted from Adam's turning away from greatest good, his will was directly involved. The flesh, as we saw in the second chapter, cannot be charged with having brought about sin because in Adam's unfallen state the body was in every respect the soul's obedient instrument. Even "Fallen Nature is not Sinfull Nature before it is Rationall nature." The effect of sin may be conspicuously evidenced in the spirit's bodily agent, but it is entirely the product of reason and will. The responsibility for Adam's Fall from grace lay in his vain will which deliberately turned away from God toward itself.

21. For a discussion of Calvin's view, see Roy W. Battenhouse, "The Doctrine of Man in Calvin and in Renaissance Platonism," *Journal of the History of Ideas*, 9 (October 1948), 455.

God's gift of free will was given to man as a part of the divine image; without it Adam simply would not have been man.[22] Consequently, while his natural and eternal life depended upon God, Adam's moral state initially depended upon his own will, upon its voluntary alignment with the divine will. Although God never necessitated or predestined sin, he allowed it as an act of this free will.[23] God "gives a permit to Satan, in this matter to bring forth his uttmost Diabolicall Subtilty" (C, p. 117). Though he may be unaware of it, Satan can do nothing except with divine permission, a point made perfectly clear throughout *Gods Determinations*.[24]

Adam chose not to conform to God's Law, hence obeying Satan in God's stead (C, pp. 66, 314). Enamored of his own power, Adam acted as if he could serve as his own end, as his own greatest good. His will voluntarily defected from God's immutable goodness and looked to itself for life, perfection, and love—an act contrary to the law of nature and, of course, to the will of God (TCLS, p. 201). Evil, above all else, is the perversion of man's ability to love. The more the will delights in self-love, in its own image of power, the more entrenched is its perversity.

The most severe outcome of this violation of the natural order was suffered by Adam and all his children, for they were deprived of God's image—that reflection of the divine loveliness which makes, among other things, the faculties harmonious and which insures the freedom of the will. This loss meant that Adam's reason and will would no longer mirror the divine order.

22. See Augustine, *On Free Choice of the Will*, 2.1.5.

23. See Thomas Hooker, *The Application of Redemption*, p. 266 and Edwards, *Freedom of the Will*, pp. 339, 409.

24. See also Calvin, *Institutes*, 1.14.17. In the light of *Gods Determinations*, which may have been influenced by *Paradise Lost*, I think Taylor would have agreed with Milton that Satan's efforts to snare Adam and Eve were intended by Providence to provide an occasion for both of them to grow in their obedient love for God. That their spiritual growth was part of the divine scheme is quite clear (see note 19 of chapter 1), and testing Adam's will and its willingness to obey was doubtless a part of God's progressive and perfect design. For a perceptive discussion of this point and related matters in Milton, see Arthur E. Barker, "Structural and Doctrinal Pattern in Milton's Later Poems," in *Essays in English Literature from the Renaissance to the Victorian Age*, ed. Miller MacLure and F. W. Watt, pp. 169–94.

His understanding, deprived of its ability to ascertain truth naturally and immediately, henceforth bore a blinded eye. Its once divine image was reduced to a shattered glass.

Likewise the will, now enslaved to improper desires, lost its ready power to choose the greatest good: "The Will is hereupon perverted so, / It laquyes after ill, doth good foregoe" (GD, p. 409). Evidencing a "stiff, stubborn, and Rebellious" state, the will "sooner breakes than buckles to fulfill / Gods Laws"; now the "Forward Will joyn'd with a froward minde" caters to temporal goods ("worldly toyes"), the price of which "is grown so deare, / They pick my purse" (GD, p. 425; 2.42, 5–6). It follows, of course, that a "Stonifide" heart generates "Flinty Affections" (1.18, 9–10).

The Fall, in short, affects the whole man, giving rise to the soul's ignorance and the body's concupiscence. Whereas formerly in the natural order of being man held fellowship with the angels, he was deprived of that relation, owing not to his flesh but to the impurity of his sinful heart.[25] For the root of sin lies in the contrariety of the will to natural law and the divine will; hence, "the Battle must be fought, where the Enemy is quarter'd, and that is in the heart" (C, p. 60).

Taylor clearly argued, however, that no action can truly thwart God's purpose or plan, a conviction which led the poet to depict sin in relation to God's act of creation. As we saw in the first chapter, Taylor made use of imagery depicting various fluids in order to suggest that in the act of creation God's gracious Being—that is to say, his love—flowed or ran from his hand (2.15, 33–34), that it subsequently pervades everything,

> filling Heaven to the brim!
> O're running it: all running o're beside
> This World! Nay Overflowing Hell.
>
> (1.1, 7–9)

25. "It is not in locality we are distant from them [the good angels], but in merit of life, caused by our miserable unlikeness to them in will, and by the weakness of our character, for the mere fact of our dwelling on earth under the conditions of life in the flesh does not prevent our fellowship with them. It is only prevented when we, in the impurity of our hearts, mind earthly things" (Augustine, *City of God*, 8.25).

This *Aqua Vitae* or love, perpetually communicated to creation by the Son, is incessantly reflected back to God by everything; and, consequently, the "Law of Nature teacheth us to love them that love us" (C, p. 31; see also p. 261).

For Taylor sin is creation retrograde; it is a parody of genesis. Because it seeks to spoil God's design or will, sin is depicted by Taylor as the backward rushing of water. Roaring "Floods out from hell" overflow the world with sin, as Satan aims "to Subvert, and overturn the Glorious Work of God in the Creation: and to run it all to ruin" (2.29, 10–12; C, p. 117). Whereas creation, like man's soul, was initially "Inlin'de with Glorious Grace up to the brim" (1.2, 15), subsequent to the Fall, the world is "all filld up to the brim / With Sins" (1.19, 7–8). Man, bereft of the creative waters of divine love or grace, finds himself in "A Pit indeed of Sin: No water's here" (2.77, 19).

Taylor's use of the terms *subvert* and *overturn* indicates that he would have fully agreed with Jonathan Edwards' interpretation of sin as "a turning of all things upside down, and the succession of a state of the most odious and dreadful confusion."[26] Both Taylor and Edwards, though their thought differs in certain other respects, refer to sin as a perversion of God's creation. God's work in the world as well as in man's body and soul now appears deprived of order and nearly seems returned to a state of chaotic nothingness. They looked upon sin as an effort to reverse or destroy the hierarchy of glory God built into nature (C, pp. 90, 159–60; TCLS, pp. 142–43). Sin is directed at "Defacing the Glory of the Creation," at bringing about "the Everlasting Ruine of Mankinde" and "the Everlasting Disgrace, and Dishonour of God" (C, p. 95).

But the divine scheme is immutable. Owing to his omniscience God anticipated man's transgression and provided for it in the design of his creation. Taylor's portrait in *Gods Determinations* of the Son's acceptance of the role of man's redeemer before creation[27] reflects God's foreknowledge, not his predestination of sin. God readily converts sin into good, for whereas good can

26. *Original Sin*, p. 382.
27. See Grabo, *Edward Taylor*, p. 162.

exist without evil, the opposite is not true; that is, as a perversion of good, sin has no other context in which to exist but goodness.[28] God makes such excellent use of evil wills that, as Taylor indicates throughout his writings, even the paragon of evil is a mere instrument of providential will. Having failed in his effort to bring man "into Eternall Disgrace, and baseness," Satan actually "occasion'd greater Grace to begrace" mankind; for the Fall, albeit no *felix culpa*, provided the means whereby man, through Christ, would achieve a "greater Advancement than otherwise he was Capable of" (C, p. 25; see also 2.44, 41–42). God transforms every wicked intention and "brings out of this Stinking thing Sweetness"; since everything must finally manifest the greater glory of the divine will, Satan's every effort to disturb God's universal order becomes self-destructive and ultimately "is made to Serve to the ruin of his [own] design, and to advance the Contrary to it" (C, p. 96). God shapes "Goodbad wayes" to suit his own ends (1.35, 21): "The Curse now Cures" (1.18, 34). In short, there exists, Taylor explains, a natural and eternal "Counterplot" to all sinful endeavors (C, p. 255). No matter how adverse to God anything may appear, it always contributes to God's original plot or plan of creation.

What these observations lead to is the significant point that sin has no objective reality. Taylor maintained the Augustinian idea that voluntary acts of the will which give birth to sin in no way actually disturb God's universal order. Sin represents only a moral agent's defection from His will and love.[29] Sin, lacking substantive existence, is solely a moral condition of the perverse will which has turned aside from the reality of God's greatest good to some lesser good. Thus, when he wrote of the underlying and pervading influence of divine wisdom in created nature that "the entrance of Sin *Seems* to vacate this Wisdom" (C, p. 312; italics added), Taylor meant that sin is devoid of any ability to interfere with the fundamental reality of creation. This is also

28. See Augustine, *Divine Providence and the Problem of Evil*, 2.7.23, and *City of God*, 11.17; Edwards, *Freedom of the Will*, pp. 408–9.

29. Augustine, *The Greatness of the Soul*, 36.80 and *Confessions*, 7.16. See also Edwards, *Religious Affections*, p. 325.

suggested by a revision he made in the Westfield "Church Record." He had at first written: "Sin therefore in it's nature is a Consequence of the Covenant of Works, consisting in any want of Conformity unto [it]." On rereading this passage Taylor carefully inserted the phrase "Spirituall Evill" after the article *a*, changing as well the next two words to read "Consequent from."[30]

Although its postlapsarian motions contribute to man's purgative process, the essence of nature remains untouched by sin. God's design is indeed inviolate. Moreover, that man has damaged the best of God's looms—that is, has brought about his own internal discord or disharmony—does not mean that his sin has in any way disrupted the "Golden Theame" or "Golden Web" of Providence (1.26, 7–10). The law of reason or nature endures untarnished in spite of man's dissent from it. Not "the least ray of Divine Providence" can be affected by the stain of sin (C, p. 117). That evil is only a subjective or mental condition is evident in Taylor's comment on men who live in sin: "while you abide in this State, You are enemies in your minds" (C, p. 224; see also, p. 60).

Taylor fashioned a great number of images to suggest that in the saint sin exists as a passing, superficial condition, that it represents a mere mental lapse from glory. At times he portrays sin as a clogging obstruction in those means (pipes) whereby man receives and expresses love (1.34, 1–2; 2.75, 19–24; C, p. 195), a condition remedied by the flow of Christ's grace. Likewise, the use of the traditional image of sin as a vile but curable disease abounds in Taylor's verse; the poet deplored that he was "All Candid o're with Leprosie of Sin" (2.3, 16; see also 2.27, 8) and that his soul languished, "sick of th' Scurvy" (2.67 [B], 11). Christ's healing grace cures all of the illnesses attending sin (2.75, 41) and provides the proper nutriment for the soul (2.108, 49–54).

Often Taylor describes sin in Pauline images suggesting a removable covering or veil, as something temporarily enveloping

30. Westfield "Church Record," p. 23. Edwards wrote: "The world was ruined, as to man, as effectually as if it had been reduced to *chaos* again" (*Works*, 1: 303).

or enshrouding the saint's jewel-like holiness. On account of the "prison robes" of sin (TCLS, p. 173), the elect are "Pearls in Puddles cover'd o're with mudd" (GD, p. 401; see also p. 431). Similarly sin is a dye coloring the soul scarlet (2.77, 23–24; cf. 2.8, 13–14), a sauce (1.31, 14), vomit on man's cheeks (1.47, 6), a black velvet mask ("The Reflexion," 40), a film over reason's eye (1.35, 39–40), ashes smothering the soul (2.49, 11–12), rust (2.54, 7), and ice encasing the affections (2.53, 2). Indeed, because fallen flesh is "with Sin all rin'de" (2.49, 16), the victimized body appears to be a "Snake like pi'de" jacket (2.69, 8).

Especially relevant to the meaning of these images is Taylor's association of sin with charms and spells, which imply that evil only temporarily captivates the soul of the saint: "Oh! what strange Charm encrampt my Heart with spite / Making my Love gleame out upon a Toy?" (1.33, 7–8; see also 2.3, 6). The answer, of course, is sin, for the will "is the very Soile / Where Satan reads his Charms, and sets his Spell" (1.40, 9–10; see also 1.43, 11). The spellbinding effect of sin becomes a "Winding Sheet" enshrouding the morally dead or loveless soul (1.25, 11–12).

But just as death is an *ad interim* enchantment and a "Pious Fraud" in regard to Christ (1.19, 13), so also the consequences of the Fall prove to be a mere transient spell cast over the saint's love, the most vital affection of his will (1.34, 38–40). Though sin banishes love (2.8, 9), "Damps" it (1.43, 3), and rusts the heart's lock behind which "Love crincht in a Corner lies" (1.42, 11) and "is but a shrimpy thing / A sorry Crickling a blasted bud" (2.161 [A], 7–8), evil never truly kills it: "Love like to hunger'll breake through stone strong Walls. / Nay brazen Walls cannot imprison it" (2.39, 7–8). The elect, driven by the will's instinctive yearning for the ultimate source of its being and animation, are awakened as the love of their hearts responds to the "Ambient Charms" of Christ's love (2.86, 3; see also 2.123 [B], 43–45; 2.142, 36). Because it never fails to "unscrew Loves Cabbinet" (1.25, 33), Christ's saving love or election[31] begets love: "let thy Loveli-

---

31. Samuel Willard says that "Election is Gods act of love" (*Some Brief Sacramental Meditations, Preparatory for Communion*, Boston, 1711, pp. 128–29).

ness, Lord touch my heart. / And let my heart imbrace thy loveliness" (2.97, 49–50); what "Desire draws in, . . . Love goes out to meet" (2.127, 12). During the ensuing regenerative process the saint's rational eye becomes increasingly illuminated and, in accord with the order of nature, his heart, tapping "True Loves Veane" (1.36, 72) and turning to Christ as "The Object of All Love" (2.127, 45; see also 2.115, 44; 2.158, 61–66; C, p. 30), subsequently undergoes conversion; for if Christ's "Glory ever kiss thine Eye, / Thy Love will soon Enchanted bee thereby" (1.12, 29–30). Since the heart is the seat or mine of love (2.12, 21; 2.116, 1–2), Christ's bewitching of this faculty necessarily includes his charming of all the affections (1.14, 45; 2.73, 51), of which love is the foundation.

Taylor usually depicts these effects of grace in musical terms. Conversion is accomplished through Christ's symphony of love or grace, which attunes man's will to that of God. It is the symphony which pervades all creation, which informs the hierarchical degrees of glory evidenced in the scale of nature, and which, as we noted in chapter 1, always points back to God: "this hath been the way His providence hath trod in universally, viz., to reserve something that is most concerning, as the *ultima lima* of glory last attained unto, as an allurement unto the most excellent accomplishments" (TCLS, p. 143). This allurement is the underlying reality of the universe; it is God's will, his infinite love. In postlapsarian times this attraction becomes a spell whenever it enables the will of a saint to *re-turn* and become God's tool (1.26, 34; 2.23, 73–78), particularly His musical instrument; for when it is in fact completely renewed in heaven, the heart finds itself in tune with the graceful/grace-full music of the divine will. Whereas formerly the heart had fallen prey to the spell of Satan's discordant and dissonant music, the saint's heart now learns again, when "God turns the Scales" (C, pp. 95–96), how to sing the correct "Gam-Ut" (1.29, 36). Hoping that the enchantment of grace would attune his will to that of God, Taylor asked God to make "My Heart thy Harp: and mine Affections brac'de / With gracious Grace thy Golden Strings" (2.54, 8–9).

In heaven even the death of the body, like sin which brought it about, will be unmasked as a transitory spell. In a tender poem entitled "Upon Wedlock, and Death of Children," Taylor explains that the enchantment of sin and death is dispelled by the magic of God's will:

> Griefe o're doth flow: and nature fault would finde
> Were not thy Will, my Spell Charm, Joy, and Gem:
> That as I said, I say, take, Lord, they're thine.
> I piecemeal pass to Glory bright in them.
> I joy, may I sweet Flowers for Glory breed,
> Whether thou getst them green, or lets them seed.

For the elect Christ has "Washt Deaths grim grim face" (1.34, 29), by unveiling the inability of sin to stain, to infest, and to enshroud the soul as well as by enticing, through the charms of grace, the saint's whole being, his body as well as his soul, to heavenly glory.

Hence for Taylor sin is a mere privation, a "Dungeon State" (2.77, 1) from which the love of the elect must be freed. It arose from and resides in the perverse will's mental rebellion against God's design, whereby everything is ordained to mirror love back to him. It is, like death, only a fraudulent, superficial perversion of an underlying and immutable reality, a passing eclipse in the saint of the true and eternal pearllike love and goodness pervading all creation. Sin constitutes a spell out of which the saints, among whom Taylor hoped to be identified, are gradually but certainly awakened by the affectionate music of Christ into his regenerating, re-creative "Sea of Electing Grace, and Love" (c, p. 305).

(b) As the preceding discussion has already suggested, since the will is the source and seat of sin—"A Nest of Vipers" (1.40, 5) in which sinful "Bubs" are hatched "on Serpents Eggs" (1.39, 3)—it must assume an equally central position in the drama of conversion. If one is to undergo the regenerative process, this faculty must become the seat or instrument of grace: "My Gracious Lord, Take thou my heart and plant / Each Sanctifying

66

Grace therein" (2.145, 31–32). To counter their disobedience the elect seek to exemplify a new obedience through a passive and an active exercise of their wills. Although the saint realizes that this new obedience will never be fully attained in the temporal life, he inevitably looks to his will or heart for signs of conversion; for God makes the heart of the saint his throne (GD, p. 413).

As we have already seen, the fact that for Taylor the heart becomes the abode of grace does not imply the circumvention of the natural hierarchy existing in the rational soul. He agreed with Calvin, however, that faith cannot be solely an intellectual experience; to be true faith it must take root in the renewed will.[32] No amount of rational knowledge indicates the condition of a man's soul, for assent of the understanding alone to divine truth comprises an insufficient response to God's call:

> What rocky heart is mine? My pincky Eyes
> Thy Grace spy blancht, Lord, in immensitie.
> But finde the Sight me not to meliorize,
> O Stupid Heart!
>
> (1.36, 1–4)

What is required is a man's entire being, and the central animating mechanism for the whole man is his will.

Like everything else in creation, as Taylor's imagery of sin suggests, the will fundamentally retains its inherent inclination toward God and its potentiality for good. To be sure, since the Fall it is unable to regulate man's being properly and it cannot turn in perfect obedience to God. As a "Pouch of Passion," as a "Swamp, Brake, Thicket vile of Sin," the heart is bereft of its willingness to rely on reason and so fails to know how to choose or act rightly (2.25, 5; 1.45, 2; GD, p. 389). The power of the will to act in harmonious obedience to God's universal order lies in his efficacious grace, the same grace which rendered Christ's "Obedience Complete Obedience" (C, p. 248).[33] Without it a

---

32. *Institutes*, 3.2.36. See also Willard, *Compleat Body*, p. 454; and Edwards, "True Grace Distinguished in the Experience of Devils," *Works*, 4: 451–73.

33. "Let me offer you in sacrifice the service of my thoughts and my tongue, but first give me what I may offer to you" (Augustine, *Confessions*, 11.2).

man's heart can perform nothing of a saving nature: "I want a power, not will to honour thee" (2.38, 18): "Pardon my faults: they're all against my Will. / I would do Well but have too little Skill" (2.138, 11–12);

> All that my Can contains, to nothing comes
> When summed up, it onely Cyphers grows
> Unless thou set thy Figures to my Sums.
>
> (2.4, 32–34)

The *figures, power,* or meaning given the will by grace constitutes the heart's renewed ability to fulfill its duty to believe in and to obey God's will as revealed in Scripture and nature (c, pp. 388–89): "Lord, make my Soule Obedient: and when so, / Thou saist Believe, make it reply, I do" (1.25, 29–30). The exercise of this belief and obedience stems, as we noted earlier, not from new faculties but from a renewed reason and will founded on divine love or grace (GD, p. 415). The faith accompanying this grace illuminates the eye of the soul, and together faith and reason undertake to sway the will to obedience:

> Oh! that I had but halfe an eye to view
> This excellence of thine, undazled: so
> Therewith to give my heart a touch anew
> Untill I quickned am, and made to glow.
>
> (2.1, 25–28)[34]

A renewed heart, of course, engenders an improved obedience (TCLS, p. 200; C, p. 314), which each saint is to model after that of Christ, the "absolute pattern of perfect Obedience" (C, p. 167).

The renewing and converting work of this grace is not depicted by Taylor in the image of a rape of the will. Although in order to convey the urgency of his desire for salvation Taylor upon occasion invited God to "ravish" his heart (2.76, 38), he usually depicted the reception of grace or divine love as a marriage of the soul to Christ; for "Weddens are the conclusions

---

34. See also Hooker, *Application of Redemption,* pp. 35–36.

made of the greatest love and richest affections which are to be found between persons" (TCLS, p. 17): "make my Heart loaded with Love ascend / Up to thyselfe, its bridegroom" (2.115, 5–6). Man's will is never forced but coaxed and wooed by Christ. As the groom, he influences and inclines the bridelike will and, in turn, the will (like any spouse in the right spirit of marriage) gives its consent. Mutual consent is required. The will must endeavor to transform its willfulness and forwardness (GD, p. 437) into a tender and loving willingness: "With all your Soul endevour allwayes then / To be espousd in heart to Christ" (2.133, 37–38).

Grace is the wedding garment for this conjugal ceremony (TCLS, p. 29).[35] It enables the soul to return to God, thereby redressing its previous aversion to him evident in its former preoccupation with lesser goods. The ability to re-turn is founded on grace's renewal of the will's freedom, for the heart is free only when, no longer the slave of sin, it most approximates its original condition in unfallen Adam. In other words, though they all at first come to Christ with ropes around their necks (GD, p. 404), the elect gain their freedom by complying with the influence of grace and by willingly serving God: "Thy Service is my Freedom Pleasure, Joy, / Delight, Bliss, Glory, Heaven on Earth" ("The Return," ll. 31–32).[36] In the correct exercise of this freedom the will discovers liberty, which endures as long as the saint continues to imitate Christ through his heart's willing obedience to God.[37]

35. For more on the meaning of the wedding garment in Taylor's work, see Grabo's introductory remarks in TCLS, pp. xi–xiii and his "Edward Taylor's Spiritual Huswifery," *PMLA*, 79 (December 1964), 554–60.

36. This seemingly paradoxical view of man's freedom is analogous to John Winthrop's differentiation between natural liberty and federal liberty; see his well-known speech before the general court (July 3, 1645) in *The Puritans: A Sourcebook of Their Writings*, ed. Perry Miller and Thomas H. Johnson, rev. ed., 1: 205–9. Winthrop notes that federal liberty not only refers to "the politic covenants and constitutions, amongst men themselves," but also may "be termed moral, in reference to the covenant between God and man, in the moral law."

37. "There be three things the Spirit helps us to in any duty we take in hand: First, ability for it: Secondly, liberty or freedome of spirit in it: Thirdly, it puts a kind of necessity upon us, that wee must needs doe it" (Cotton, *The Way of Life*, p. 9).

It is important from Taylor's point of view not to confuse consent with mere acquiescence. To be sure, in the matters of election and the reception of grace man is totally passive; Taylor declared in the Westfield "Church Record" that "the Principall of the Souls returning to God is the passive principle of Grace wrought upon the Will by the free grace of God."[38] In his marriage with the soul, however, Christ seeks an "active and passive obedience unto the Law" (c, p. 98; see also 2.160, 21–22). Since he never forces the consent of the chosen, Christ "must waite their Will" (GD, p. 395).[39]

Everything in creation instructs the heart to make this consent: "The whole Creation doth bring all its Shining Glory, as a Sacrifice to be offerd up to God from, and upon the Altar of the Rationall Creature in Sparkling Songs of praises to God" (c, p. 312). God made everything "according to His own holy will on purpose to bring men off from their sins if they will approve themselves to God therein" (TCLS, p. 124). The *if* implies that some sort of active effort must arise from man's will, for in order for Christ's election or marriage of a soul to be a true covenant, the saint must exercise his will's renewed freedom in choosing Christ in return. This concept underlies Taylor's frequent pleas for grace: "Accept of mee, and make mee thee accept" (2.43, 51); it informed his view of the means by which the elect would eventually secure eternal life, for they are to imitate Christ's "Obedience prime" which "Active, and Passive is the Food that all / That have this Life feed on" (2.81, 28–30).

This passive and active obedience may be said to include two phases: the full consent of one's will and the free, deliberate

38. Westfield "Church Record," p. 45.

39. Willard taught that man's chief duty is obedience and conformity to God's revealed will in a passive and an active service (*Compleat Body*, pp. 559–62). In "A Divine and Supernatural Light," Edwards similarly remarks that though a saint's faculties are the object of grace, "they are the subject in such a manner, that they are not merely passive, but active in it" (*Works*, 4: 433). Just as they agree on the place of the body in God's plan, so are Taylor and Donne in accord concerning the passive and active role of the will in conversion. Donne wrote that the power of the heart to act is passively received from God, but it is "from God in a diverse manner, and a diverse respect; and certainly our works are more ours then our faith is " (*Sermons*, 10: 89).

willing of God's will. There exists at best a thin, almost negligible distinction between these two stages, and I am being somewhat arbitrary in arguing their difference. But it is helpful to approach the subject in this manner in order to understand better Taylor's focus on the heart's response to grace. The heart, in submitting to its inclination, must recognize Christ as its Captain and accept his will as its guide (GD, p. 405). By means of grace the will returns from its sinful dissent from Being or God and, with renewed power, consents to the greatest good, God's will. Consent means a willing, somewhat passive acceptance of God's Law. It involves the yielding or submission of the saint's will to God's will.[40] This consent leads to a conformity of the converted will to that of God; for grace "Will Subdue" the "Wills and Affections" of the elect, thereby leading them to "a conformity unto Christ in all his divine ordinance and institutions" (C, p. 399; TCLS, p. 183).[41] In brief, the saint must be able to say truly with Christ, "Thy Will be done" (2.40, 12).

When the will passively consents and conforms to the divine will, it shares to some limited extent in that will and hence regains sufficient freedom enabling it to offer more than mere consent. In spite of the fact that this renewed capacity for action remains firmly rooted in the soul's initial passivity, the heart can now forcefully *will* God's design.[42] Thus Taylor wrote: "Give me, Lord, Life and Grace to boot then I / Will give My Life and Selfe to thee" (2.87, 41–42). The saint must experience this desire to collaborate actively with God's will: "Will thy Will, I must, or must / From Heavens sweet Shine to Hells hot flame be thrust" (1.16, 11–12). He must always consciously seek a person-

40. Hooker tried to explain this effect: "God leaves a powerful impression upon the will, acts this capability to carry it from sin in a right order to God; at the entrance of which, the soul is moved, and takes the impression or motion, it moves again, and in virtue of that is said to act and consent, so that this consent is not from our selves, though not without our selves" (*The Application of Redemption*, pp. 395–96).

41. See also Reynolds, *A Treatise of the Passions*, p. 113; Baxter, *The Saints Everlasting Rest*, p. 174; Willard, *Compleat Body*, p. 564.

42. Dwarfed by its passive reliance on grace, the power of the saint's will is too often overlooked. In "Edward Taylor's *Preparatory Meditations:* A Decorum of Imperfection," for example, Charles W. Mignon writes of a "will-killing decorum" and a "will-paralyzed conscience" (pp. 1427, 1428).

al role in the fulfillment of God's plan. Just as truth (the object of reason) consists of the agreement of man's ideas with those of God, good (the object of the will) lies in the conformity of the heart to the divine will. The imagery of the following passages suggests this intimate and inseparable union between the two wills: "such blest Sight [of reason] shall twist my heart with thine" (2.74, 41); "Drill through my metall-heart an hole wherein / With graces Cotters to thyselfe it pin" (1.49, 5–6);

> And let thy Scepter drill my heart in mee:
> And let thy Spirits Cotters pierce it through
> Like golden rivits, Clencht, mee hold to thee.
> Then thou and I shall ne'er be separate.
>
> (2.53, 44–47)

For Taylor this conformity of the wills represents the final work of converting grace. Thus, in response to the lamentations of the saints in *Gods Determinations*, Christ says, "Anchor thy heart on mee thy Rock" (p. 418). Everywhere in Taylor's poetry the will is exhorted to consent and to conform to God's will as its captain.

The ability to consent and to conform arises from the regenerative process, which remains unfulfilled during the saint's earthly life. In order to avoid violating a man's will, God makes this drama of conversion progressive—a notion, incidentally, in harmony with Taylor's concept of God's continuous creation: "The Reall Change of State is a progressive renewall of the Qualities of man in the likeness of God."[43] In spite of the sea of grace (C, p. 305), therefore, the saint continues to experience amidst the "Worlds wild waves" (2.111, 12) an ebb and flow of his hope between the two shores of presumption and despair.[44] Often the poems of the *Preparatory Meditations* open with a sense

43. Westfield "Church Record," p. 51. Michael J. Colacurcio offers some insight on this point in Taylor's work in "*Gods Determinations Touching Half-Way Membership*: Occasion and Audience in Edward Taylor," *American Literature*, 39 (November 1967), 307. John Cotton did not stress this aspect; but in speaking of "the approach that we are dayly making towards God," he taught that "we are every day to turne to God, for conversion is a continued act"; "build up yourselves in your most holy faith" (*The Way of Life*, pp. 205, 341, 342). Everett Emerson has suggested that Calvin allowed for the gradual process of regeneration ("Calvin and Covenant Theology," p. 140).

44. See Taylor's "The Ebb and Flow." Elsewhere Taylor explains that he is "tost up

of despair and close with intimations of renewal and hope. Likewise *Gods Determinations* recounts this response in the elect; though spiritually anchored in Christ, they still experience in their daily lives a sense of drifting between the lure of Satan's perverse, disdainful logic and the assurances conveyed in Christ's promises. In this manner the saints experience the progressive work of grace. Just as God never abandons his creation but continues to will, reassert, and govern it at every moment, he never deserts the soul which has been reborn or re-created by grace but maintains a constant renewing influence: "Be ever, Lord beginning till I end, / At carrying on thine Intrest in my Soule" (2.38, 43–44).

This interpretation of the power of grace is reflected in Taylor's understanding of Christ's human presence on earth. If he were truly man and if he is indeed to serve as fallen man's exemplar of the new obedience arising from grace, then Christ must also have experienced some sense of this progressive ebb and flow. He was, to be sure, free from the possibility of sinning; yet, according to Taylor, Christ learned to exercise his obedience to the Father in the midst of real human conditions. Consequently, in spite of the fact that "the Humane Hall" of his body was "furnished with all Ripe Grace," still it was "Not all ore Window, that no beame at all / Of further light could have into it pass"; rather, as man Christ "learnd Obedience in his Suff'ring-Schoole. / Experience taught him (though a Feeble toole)" (2. 41, 25–36).

Taylor realized, of course, that only after death and in heaven did the saint finally achieve a full obedience to God. For only then would the body be perfected and the faculties of the soul be endowed with complete renewed harmony. Nevertheless, because it is the most vital faculty in the regenerate regulation of his "Person" or whole being (2.90, 63–66), Taylor looked to the temporal exercise of his will for a sign of his salvation, "In hope of Which I in thy Service sing / Unto thy Praise upon my Harp

---

and down" in regard to religious experience (Stanford, "Edward Taylor's 'Spiritual Relation,' " p. 473).

within" (2.17, 53–54).[45] In response to conversion the will, as we saw in the preceding section, is enchanted by God and becomes his musical instrument—a "Shoshannim" with well-tuned strings (2.69, 42; 2.101, 60), a musical pipe (2.7, 40; 2.110, 37), a bagpipe (2.129, 29), a golden trumpet (2.54, 31), a "Cittern" with the affections serving as its "wyers" (2.110, 49–50):

> My Breast, be thou the ringing Virginalls:
> Ye mine Affections, their sweet Golden Strings,
> My Panting Heart, be thou for Stops, and Falls:
> Lord, let thy quick'ning Beams dance o're the Pins.
> Then let thy Spirit this sweet note resume,
> ALTASCHATH MICHTAM, in Seraphick Tune.
>
> (1.18, 43–48)

> Be thou Musician, Lord, Let me be made
> The well tun'de Instrument thou dost assume.
> And let thy Glory be my Musick plaide.
> Then let thy Spirit keepe my Strings in tune.
>
> ("The Return," 49–52)

As the final line of the last quotation makes clear, the Spirit maintains the conformity of man's will to that of God by means of grace, which gift serves with the affections as the strings or wires of the heart (2.102, 41; 2.136, 47). In a common procedure for Taylor (to be discussed in a later chapter), the musical harmony arising from conversion or grace's attunement of the saint's will to the divine will involves a circular relation. Joined in a bond of love to which both have consented, the will of the saint and that of God share a "mutuall Intrest" (2.35, 11). The converted will in some sense partakes of the divine will: "I am thine, and thou art mine indeed. / Propriety is mutuall" (2.69, 38–39). Consequently, if the poet is elected not only does his heart

45. See also 2.9, 59–60; 2.54, 54. The image is derived from the Psalms. Baxter refers to the will in the same manner: "The soul that is best furnished with grace, when it is not in action, is like a lute well stringed and tuned, which while it lieth still makes no more music than a common piece of wood; but when it is handled by a skillful musician, the melody is delightful" (*The Saints Everlasting Rest*, p. 163).

become God's musical instrument, but one which God plays in praise of himself: "Thy joyes in mee will make my Pipes to play / For joy thy Praise" (1.48, 41–42);

> Oh! that my Heart, thy Golden Harp might bee
> Well tun'd by Glorious Grace, that e'ry string
> Screw'd to the highest pitch, might unto thee
> All Praises wrapt in sweetest Musick bring.
>
> ("The Experience," 25–28)

This notion of the reciprocal relationship between Christ and the saint as well as the image of circularity which it informs suggest that Taylor may have been intentionally ambiguous in regard to the specific reference for the word *harp* in the following lines: "My little mite of Love shall musick sweet / Tune forth on thee, its harp, that heaven shall greet" (2.97, 53–54). In some sense the saint's will and the divine will are instrumental to each other, a very important point to bear in mind when considering Taylor's poetic decorum (chapter 5).

Such imagery is appropriate for showing the effects of the attunement of the saint's will to that of God because music conveys meaning beyond reason and elicits the response of the heart.[46] Music provided Taylor with an image which communicates the sense of the nature of God's gracious enchantment. For Taylor music was a symbol for the reestablished harmony of the regenerate faculties, of the renewed relation between the body and the soul, of the conversion of a man's heart, and of that vital, essential alignment—thought to exist in a state of music—of all created nature with God.[47] The regenerative process should produce in the hearts of the elect a sense of this musical relation of all things. With his will thus graciously tuned, the saint's entire being, body and soul, again mirrors the divine image; and his will then becomes a musical instrument on which God plays in praise of himself.

46. Consider, for instance, John Dryden's "A Song for St. Cecilia's Day" and "Alexander's Feast."

47. The belief that the universe is pervaded with divine music is, of course, an old one; see E. M. Tillyard, *The Elizabethan World Picture*, p. 94.

Thus, Taylor struggled in his meditations to achieve momentary and fleeting experiences, albeit not mystically, of the divine music pervading everything and especially underlying the conversion or attunement of the saint's will to the divine will. In the intimate words brought forth through the passive disposition and active exercise of his heart he hoped to catch a glimpse of the moral state of his whole being, of whether or not his will was the musical instrument of God and the featherbed of faith.

iii

Christian tradition associates the will with the Holy Spirit and with the affection of love. Sanctifying grace or divine love—terms, we should bear in mind, which Taylor used as synonyms for life or being—represents "the Trade winde of the Holy Ghost" (2.64, 18; see also TCLS, p. 16); the will, then, becomes "tun'de by" the "Spirits Skill" (2.54, 12). Punning on the literal meanings of *spirit*—*breathe* and *blow*; by metonymy, *bellows* and *gale*—Taylor asks Christ to "Breath" into his soul "the Realm of Life" (2.39, 33), for it is the Spirit's breath which revives the heart (2.30, 69–70): "let thy Spirits breath, as Bellows, blow / That this new kindled Life may flame and glow" (2.82, 17–18; see also 2.49, 11). In order to enjoy the "gales of Graces breath" (2.130, 43), one's heart must be driven "sweetly by Gailes of the Holy Ghost" (2.78, 35).

Moreover, not only did he designate the will as the object of the work of God's Spirit, but Taylor reflects Augustinian reasoning in the analogy he draws between each man's will and the third Person of the Trinity.[48] In fact, like other Puritan ministers, Taylor held that the infusion of grace in the heart is accomplished by the union of the Spirit with this faculty: "let thy boundless Love my Lord, a Kiss / Bestow on me and joyn me to thy Dove" (2.141, 37–38). The will

48. See Augustine, *The Trinity*, 9.5.8; 15.21.41. The best study of Puritan thought on the Holy Spirit is Geoffrey F. Nuttall, *The Holy Spirit in Puritan Faith and Experience*.

thereby gains a renewed foundation by means of which it can properly function with reason, hence more rightly integrating and regulating the whole man. In short, the Holy Spirit dwells in the will of the saint.

To portray the residence of the Holy Spirit in the heart, Taylor poetically expanded the traditional identification of the Spirit as a dove, thereby deriving a motif comprised of recurring images of birds, feathers, wings, nests, roosting, hatching, and eggs. Fallen man, deprived of the Spirit's presence, laments that "Soule Sicknesses do nest in mee" (2.69, 10), that "Humane Wisdom's hatcht within the nest / Of addle brains" (2.95, 11–12), that his soul's "Gold-Finch Angell Feathers [are] dapled in / Hells Scarlet Dy fat, blood red grown with Sin" (2.77, 23–24), and that his soul has become "A Nest of Vipers" (1.40, 5) in which sinful "Bubs" are hatched "on Serpents Eggs" (1.39, 3). He forlornly asks, "Shall loves nest be a thorn bush?" (1.48, 10).

The answer lies in the saint's heart, the reclaimed nest of the Holy Spirit. When sheltered "under loves Wing" the saint is joined with God's dove and is enabled by love to coo his praise (2.141, 43–48). This love was first "hatcht in heaven of an heavenly Egge / The Holy Ghost layd there in'ts feather bed" (2. 165, 11–12). But in accordance with God's design this affection and the faith accompanying it seek another "Feather Bed," the wills of the elect (2.155, 37). There "Graces Egg layst in their very hearts / Hatchest and brudl'st in this nest" (2.111, 7–8; see also c, p. 371). It is in the will, as the center of the whole man, that the Spirit hatches the "Spring of Life" (2.126, 7–8), a renewed life founded on love and reclaiming the entire soul. As a result of this "Spring of Life," reason, "Where Swallows build, and hatch: Sins black and red," is transformed into "Graces Dovehouse turret"; and the will, formerly the nest of sin, serves as the roosting place where the Spirit gives birth to obedience (1.44, 25–34). In short, the two powers of the rational soul as well as the body partake of the new life engendered by the Spirit's grace in the converted will.

As some of the quotations cited in the preceding paragraph

make clear, the Holy Spirit is identified with pure love. This is the idea behind Taylor's depiction of love as "a flock of Doves with feathers washt, / All o're with yellow gold" (2.8, 13–14). He inherited this view, of course, from Christian tradition, according to which the Holy Spirit represents the love generated between the Father as lover and the Son as beloved.[49] During creation the Father, through the Word and in the Spirit, established universal love. In fact, since it stems from God's will, by which "all things are carried on" (C, p. 115), love, as we saw in chapter 1, becomes the universal cement or foundation of being (2.71, 38–39), both that of the Trinity as well as that of created nature. God's love pervades all creation, comprises that Being which everything essentially shares with God, and is what sin parodies. This love, perpetually communicated to creation by God, is incessantly reflected back to him, for the "Law of Nature teacheth us to love them that love us" (C, p. 31; see also p. 261).

Love, inseparable from Being and thus pervading all creation, unifies the spiritual and temporal realms in a fashion similar to the will's integration of the soul and the body of each man. Specifically it is the Spirit, as manifested in and through Christ, which serves as the vehicle uniting the two realms; the Holy Spirit embodies God's will and endlessly communicates his love to creation.[50] A man chosen by Christ receives the Spirit's continuous and progressive "Sea of Electing Grace, and Love," thereby enabling him both to assent—the soul's eye is "love's Pursevant" (2.116, 7)—and to consent to the divine will. Since this "Spirit of Grace is graciously distilld" by the heat of God's loving will (1.7, 3–4), its reception becomes for the saint an experience of love in his heart;[51] the converted will partakes of the Spirit's loving nature: "Thy rapid flames my Love enquicken will" (2.73, 52).

Since the will represents the whole man, its chief affection,

49. See Augustine, *The Trinity*, 8.10.14; 15.17.31.

50. See Augustine, *Confessions*, 4.4; and *Edwards on the Trinity*, p. 111.

51. This point is clear in Taylor's "Spiritual Relation." In *Religious Affections*, Edwards notes that love is both a particular affection and the foundation of all the other affections (pp. 106, 113). See also Reynolds, *A Treatise of the Passions*, p. 74.

love, is equally representative; and if a man truly loves God, he necessarily dedicates his whole being to conforming to God's will. Having enlightened the understanding and taken up residence in the heart, the Spirit affects the soul's bodily agent by means of the faculties of the rational soul. It enables the whole man to respond in love to divine love:

> Oh! let thy Beauty give a glorious tuch
> Upon my Heart, and melt to Love all mee.
> Lord melt me all up into Love for thee.
>
> (1.12, 45–47)

This affection provides the most important sign of the Spirit's converting work in the saint's will.

The outcome of this love is the will's movement away from a preoccupation with itself (pride) and toward a devotion to God (charity). This effect is brought about by grace's renewal of the divine image in the soul. More and more the saint's heart must be able to consent lovingly in a harmonious response to the assent of reason to God's revealed will. Love must dwell "Within the heart, where thron'd, without Controle / It ruleth all the Inmates of the Soule" (2.66, 5–6). Ultimately, in heaven, the findings of reason will be inseparable from the will's acts of love. There the saint's body will likewise demonstrate complete obedience to the rational soul and reflect outwardly this internal condition. But while on earth, the saint's whole being will progress by degrees through charitable action directed particularly toward the good of others as well as generally and finally toward God's greatest goodness.

If Taylor's primary focus is indeed on the human will, then his underlying theme concerns the affection of love, the expression of which the saint seeks to discover and experience during the regenerative process. Everything Taylor considers in his verse finally points to this quest for saving love or conversion, and it is significant that the first poem of the *Preparatory Meditations* directly introduces this theme:

What Love is this of thine, that Cannot bee
   In thine Infinity, O Lord, Confinde,
Unless it in thy very Person see,
   Infinity, and Finity Conjoyn'd?
   What hath thy Godhead, as not satisfide
   Marri'de our Manhood, making it its Bride?

Oh, Matchless Love! filling Heaven to the brim!
   O're running it: all running o're beside
This World! Nay Overflowing Hell; wherein
   For thine Elect, there rose a mighty Tide!
   That there our Veans might through thy Person bleed,
   To quench those flames, that else would on us feed.

Oh! that thy Love might overflow my Heart!
   To fire the same with Love: for Love I would.
But oh! my streight'ned Breast! my Lifeless Sparke!
   My Fireless Flame! What Chilly Love, and Cold?
   In measure small! In Manner Chilly! See.
   Lord blow the Coal: Thy Love Enflame in mee.

Since this poem and those it anticipates celebrate the Lord's Supper, their mutual theme necessarily relates to, among other matters, the Incarnation, when the Son wedded man to himself in a personal union; this union, a paradigm for all marriages, is founded on a covenant of perfect love. Taylor doubtless concluded that just as this manifestation of God's love cannot be properly distinguished from his will (both are manifested in the Spirit), so also each man's heart remains inseparable from his love.[52] Love provides the inherent motivation of the will as it does everything else in the universe. Thus, the condition of the will can be ascertained by the quality of the love it bears, an idea at the root of Taylor's concept of sin and his quest for conversion.

52. Allan I. Ludwig has observed that in Puritan tombstone engraving the image of a heart symbolizes, among other meanings, the love of the soul for God (*Graven Images: New England Stonecarving and Its Symbols, 1650–1815*, pp. 69, 155).

iv

Taylor maintained, as did Augustine, that the "internal holiness" (meditation, contemplation) of the renewed faculties of the rational soul is finally to become indistinct from the "external holiness" (action) of the saint's social conduct of life (TCLS, p. 167).[53] This point deserves brief comment here because it touches not only on Taylor's concept of the will but also, as chapter 5 will show, on his poetic imagery. Taylor did not interpret this idea to mean that a visible holiness reveals or determines the state of a man's soul (TCLS, p. 124). He did acknowledge, however, that a renovated reason and will would necessarily express themselves through the soul's bodily instrument. Since the body's motions derive from their relation to the will, they convey some idea of the state of the soul. Contingent on any internal harmony is an "Outward Compliance" consisting of "an holy Life, which is the Sweet blossomings of the inward Graces" (C, p. 390).[54] Another way to look at this matter would be to recall that though the Covenant of Grace fulfilled the Covenant of Works, in the opinion of some Puritan divines aspects of the latter were never entirely abrogated. In accordance with God's progressive law of nature, the Covenant of Grace supersedes and includes the older Covenant.[55]

Taylor taught that both Scripture and nature instructed every man to be engaged in some social occupation for which he possesses a special talent: "it's the product of nature's law to desire to be imployed in the best imployment" (TCLS, p. 24). Wherever he looks in the world man cannot escape the observation that God has "Set every Species in the Scale of Nature a Work" (C,

53. "The peace of the body then consists in the duly proportioned arrangement of its parts. The peace of the irrational soul is the harmonious repose of the appetites, and that of the rational soul the harmony of knowledge and action" (Augustine, *City of God*, 19.13; also *The Trinity*, 12.3.21).

54. In *Religious Affections* Edwards wrote: "the power of godliness is exerted in the first place within the soul, in the sensible, lively exercise of gracious affections there. Yet the principle of this power of godliness, is in these exercises of holy affections that are practical" (p. 450).

55. See Miller, *New England Mind*, 1: 384 and *Errand into the Wilderness*, p. 82.

p. 23). Everyone has a vocation; even Adam was not exempt from this principle. He was obliged to grow spiritually and physically; his vocation or "Speciall Dutie" was "to improove all his admirable Qualifications, and his so much to be admired at Person in the most advantageous way possible to his present State" (C, p. 116).

Adam's successors are likewise to seek proper employment in the service of God. Each person receives two vocations, one general and the other particular. The general calling includes all men and obliges them to dedicate their entire being to God's will. The particular calling concerns the affairs of the contemporary world; "tho' it is to be subservient to the other, because Man is to be ultimately bound for the Glory of God: But because it is that wherein the Man is to uphold his present Subsistence, and be Beneficial in his Generation to Mankind, it so hath a reference to this Life."[56] The "condition of God's children here in this life" is that they "are betrusted with the concerns of families, towns, and public duties"; it is plainly God's will that they manage these matters pertaining to their particular vocations, even though this attention may elicit "from them all a thousand thoughts for one bestowed upon spiritual things, save in a transient way" (TCLS, pp. 153–54). Ideally, of course, meditation on spiritual matters would influence and inform these numerous temporal concerns.

There always existed in Puritan culture this emphasis on the right use of earthly things. Other than God, nothing is to be enjoyed for itself. Everything is to be used to aid the saint in his journey toward heaven.[57] This use of earthly things should, of

56. Willard, *Compleat Body*, p. 691; also p. 653. See also Gerhard T. Alexis, "Jonathan Edwards and the Theocratic Ideal," *Church History*, 35 (September 1966), 337. The excellent studies of Max Weber (*The Protestant Ethic and the Spirit of Capitalism*, trans. Talcott Parsons) and Michael Walzer (*The Revolution of the Saints: A Study in the Origins of Radical Politics*) make clear just how the notion of an active life informed Puritan ethics. See also William Haller, *The Rise of Puritanism*, p. 123.

57. "The whole temporal dispensation was made by divine Providence for our salvation. We should use it, not with an abiding but with a transitory love and delight like that in a road or in vehicles or in other instruments, or, if it may be expressed more accurately, so that we love those things by which we are carried along for the sake of that toward which we are carried" (Augustine, *On Christian Doctrine*, trans. D. W. Robertson, 1.35.39).

course, conform to natural law, whereby everything innately turns toward God. All lesser goods must be subordinated as instruments of God's greatest good. In fact, the degree of goodness in anything depends on the degree to which it conforms to God's will. I linger over this point because too often we fail to realize that, just as with their views of the human body, the Puritans looked directly at their world. Early New England Puritans, reflecting Augustinian tradition, focused more on right action and the proper use of earthly things than on repression and denial; John Cotton thus wrote that "to keep the heart in *good order*," one must endeavor "ever to have right ends, to use right meanes to attain those ends, to have a right measure and degree of every thing; we may indeed set our hearts on the blessings of this life, yet so, as therein we doe Gods will."[58] In imitation of Christ each man is to exercise charitably his particular vocation through the active performance of his duty in this world.

Since "None can carry on what they are not capable of," it follows that "Everyone must be fitt for what they are calld to" (C, p. 92). Consequently, any refusal to comply with one's vocation entails the perversion of a divinely endowed special talent. This rejection lies in the will, the seat of disobedience. The will "is all that can be directly and immediately required by command; and other things only indirectly, as connected with the will."[59] Accepting his vocation involves both the passive and the active consent of a man's will to that of God. Hence, the conformity of the heart to the divine will, through its obedient acceptance and exercise of the vocation Providence has ordained, comprises the radical foundation of "the best Service to God that Can be done" (C, p. 169).

Because the will is the faculty chiefly engaged in this response to God's general and particular callings, Taylor associated this faculty with hearing imagery. Just as reason represents the eye of the soul, the will may be said to serve as its

---

58. Cotton, *The Way of Life*, p. 207; also pp. 270–73. In *The New England Mind*, Miller cites Cotton Mather as follows: "To study the nature and course, and use of all Gods works, is a duty imposed by God upon all sorts of men" (1: 212).

59. Edwards, *Freedom of the Will*, p. 310.

spiritual ears.[60] It should be noted, however, that at times Taylor linked the heart to the eye, as when, for example, he asked Christ to enlighten his "hearts dim Eye" (2.121, 32). Actually this image merely underlines the inseparable union of the understanding and the will; inasmuch as reason provides the means for the influence of grace on the will, it serves as the eye of the heart. However, Taylor did not usually interchange the imagery associated with these powers and most often distinctly refers to reason as the "Souls piert Eye" and to the will as its "Circumcised Eare" (2.125, 37; see also GD, pp. 406–7).

During regeneration both faculties are affected by grace; the eye of the soul is illuminated and its ear made to hear: "Thy Curled Rayes, Lord, make mine Eare Picker / To Cure my Deafeness" (2.67 [B], 55–56); "Drop into its Eares delight / Saying Return, Return my Shulamite" (2.146, 27). This depiction of the will as the ear of the rational soul is closely associated with our earlier comments concerning Taylor's reliance on the imagery of music to convey a sense of the sought-after attunement of the saint's will to the divine will. The saint's heart both hears and serves as an instrument in God's symphony of love. Failure to hear or refusal to obey the vocation to contribute to God's music ends in a dire outcome: "Every Soule, that will not heare him shall be destroyed. How should it otherwise choose"? (C, p. 70).

If, on the other hand, the saint's will has truly heard God's call, it responds in mental and physical action which conforms to God's will. Thus attuned, man's will reflects its relation to the divine will by imposing order on chaos. Whereas God created orders of being out of nothing, the wills of the elect, as God's instrumental agents, were thought to be divinely empowered to derive order out of New England's physical and moral wil-

---

60. In his discussion of metaphor, Peacham observes, "From the hearing are diverse translations taken, not so much serving to signifie the powers of the mind, as to express the affection of the heart" (*The Garden of Eloquence*, p. 5). Baxter must have agreed, for he wrote concerning the elect that "they will hear thy voice speaking to their hearts" (*The Saints Everlasting Rest*, p. 150). The tradition is quite old, and even Augustine favored the sense of hearing over that of seeing (*Confessions*, 10.26), which is appropriate in the light of his emphasis on the will; see also *City of God*, 11.2 and *On Christian Doctrine*, 1.3.4.

derness.[61] It was with this perspective in mind, among others, and with a sense of a collective will that New England Puritans developed their idea of a social covenant. From their point of view society's order or lack of it represented the external manifestation of their collective will's allegiance to or dissociation from the design of Providence. Seeking a conformity to God's plan, they imposed an order on their society which attempted to duplicate microcosmically the divine macrocosmic hierarchical scheme. By means of absolute obedience to authority each person would become more capable of disciplining his corrupt heart.

The individual will of each citizen is involved in this social relation in another significant sense as well. Just as he is to consent to God's election, were he so called, he is also consciously to choose his membership in the social covenant and to participate actively in the community. Puritans interpreted the social contract, insofar as it assured its members the freedom to exercise just rights, in the same light as that in which they saw a man's conformity to God's will: both engendered liberty. In both relations, as John Winthrop explained in his address before the General Court in 1645, a man is as free as the degree to which his will clings to a more holy will. He is most free when his will adheres and conforms to that of God.

Within this community every citizen responds to his vocation in thought, word, and deed, each of which, as we shall observe in detail in the following chapter, represents a mode of expression for the will. These three responses, like the will itself, represent the work of the whole man. In his desire to respond to God's call with his whole being, Taylor asked Christ, "Give me thy Power to work, and thou shalt finde / Thy Work attended with my hand, and minde" (2.35, 59–60). God's grace would provide the antidote to the poison Satan injects into fallen man's heart and thereby into its response in thought, word, and deed (2.67 [B], 20–21). Through the gracious renewal of the divine image

---

61. Walzer explains that through the self-discipline of "continuous, organized, methodical activity" the Puritans "sought desperately to separate themselves from the chaotic sinfulness that they imagined to surround them" (*The Revolution of the Saints*, p. 209).

in his entire being, the saint gains a "New Heart" with "New thoughts, New Words, New Wayes" (1.30, 47; see also 2.15, 35–36; 2.99, 52).[62]

Though in general Puritans were never certain that charitable thoughts, words, and deeds truly signified one's redemption, they tended to regard them as likely indicators of an internal regenerative process. Just as a "tree is known by its fruite," so also "Everyone is known by his worke" (c, p. 53). Taylor believed that men could achieve some sense of assurance concerning their election when the testimony of the heart "witnesseth with Gods Spirit & this in two ways: 1. By inward tokens, as sorrow for sin, faith in Christ . . . Love of Righteousness, & Praying for pardon. 2. By outward fruits, as a holy life, and Conversation."[63] Taylor explained this point further when he wrote that "the Excellency of Morall actions flows into the Actions from the Excellency of the Morall Qualifications of the Agent"; "The Actions wrought by the Concrete flowing from the form which is the Abstract, are not onely ascribed to the Concrete, but they are ascribed to the Concrete, as rightly bearing the name of the Abstract upon them, as just things are done by a just man, Holy things for holy men" (c, p. 464).

Yet, as his poems readily reveal, this sort of assurance is not easily discovered and rarely, if ever, maintained while the saint lives on earth. Man's moral frailty makes it exceedingly difficult for him to ascertain his own spiritual condition with any degree of comfortable certainty. Thus the saint frequently falls short of a full awareness of his election: "Such as enjoy thy Love, may lack the Sense / May have thy love and not loves evidence" (2.96, 29–30). In fact, a sustained sense of assurance based on his

---

62. Willard (*Compleat Body*, p. 563) and Mather (*The Mystery of Christ*, p. 173) both specifically stress these three responses of the will. And John Cotton remarks: "the workes of our hands, and the words of our mouths, come all from a well kept heart, that is a good will," the heart "being the fountaine of our thoughts, and words, and waies" (*The Way of Life*, pp. 201, 213).

63. Proposition six: "Whether or no a man may Be assured in this life he is Elected," in Taylor's "Theological Notes" (ms, Redwood Athenaeum, Newport, Rhode Island), p. 27[r], "By the dispensation of outward things, indeed we can neither know [God's] love or hatred, but otherwise one may" (p. 27[v]).

good works may actually mean that a man's heart is enmeshed in a net of pride and has unwittingly fallen prey to the doctrine that good works merit grace: "Whosoever trust doth to his golden deed / Doth rob a barren Garden for a Weed" (GD, p. 396). The threat of hypocrisy lurks everywhere, and at least one Puritan argued that human appearances can even deceive angels.[64] Consequently, although Puritans tended to rely more and more on practical piety as a testament of the soul's moral state, Taylor maintained a less certain view of it. He held that one's deeds, those fruits of the will, most likely do reveal the state of a man's soul—and this is an essential point in regard to his poetry—but that most men are unable to discern their true meaning. Such insight remains beyond the ability of anyone still in the process of regeneration. In God's perfect vision, however, a man's actions do indeed represent the moral condition of his soul and, subsequently, at the final judgment each person will answer for the works he has performed on earth (1.22, 34).

Despite their belief that good works do not necessarily betoken a holy will and in no way merit grace, New England Puritans developed a curious notion of the value of preparing for grace. According to this idea each person was to act *as if*, in the event that he were eventually destined to undergo regeneration, practical piety would facilitate the converting work of the Spirit in the heart. In fact, not to prepare for conversion is a sin. Possibly echoing Augustine, Taylor thus instructed his parishioners, "if you have not that Saving grace as yet, yet if you endeavour to have your Lives run forth into gracious exercise, you are in the ready way to have grace and glory too. O then Strive after a life of Grace" (C, p. 263).[65] In *Gods Determinations* Taylor explains the spirit in which one is to perform this duty of preparation:

---

64. John Cotton, *The Covenant of Grace: Discovering the Great Work of a Sinners Reconciliation to God*, pp. 58–80.

65. "Yet are they not hereupon to grow negligent, as if they were not bound to perform any duty unless upon a special motion of the Spirit; but they ought to be diligent in stirring up the grace of God that is in them" (Westminster Confession, 16.3).

Do all Good Works, work all good things you know
As if you should be sav'd for doing so.
Then undo all you've done, and it deny
and on a naked Christ alone rely.

(p. 444)

I think it is evident, without exploring the observation in detail, that this conception of the works of the heart, particularly the idea of preparing for grace through the performance of pious acts, inspired the practical applications which conclude most Puritan sermons. The nonelect as well as the chosen are to exercise their collective will in a social context, a concept pertinent to our later discussion of Taylor's view of his poetry. Everyone is to fulfill his individual talents in some proper employment and to make his particular vocation the occasion for good works in response to God's general calling.

Early New England Puritans were inspired by the hope of founding the New Jerusalem, an ideal which could be realized only by an active conformity of the entire community to the divine will. The Puritan state became a whole man in the sense that it deemed Christ as its head and citizens as its body; and just as regeneration required the conversion of a man's entire being, the establishment of God's society on earth demanded that the entire community, organized in a harmonious hierarchy, be solely dedicated to God. Likewise, an analogy was drawn from the Puritan belief that a man's piety may testify to the conversion of his will: any manifestation of moral and physical order achieved in mutual love through the works of its members might mean that the Holy Spirit dwelt in the collective will of their community.

v

Eventually segments of Puritan culture emphasized the role of the will's works to an heretical degree. But for Taylor orthodoxy was the rule. First, he enlarged upon Augustinian views of the importance of reason and the will in the drama of conversion. When reason is illuminated by that faith which accompanies the infusion of saving grace, then the truth that faculty perceives is conveyed to the will. It is the will which remains central in Taylor's thought. To this faculty he attributed the integration of the body and the soul, an integration making the heart representative of the whole man. Second, he taught that it was Adam's will which proved to be pivotal in the Fall, at which time it was transformed into the seat of sin. Consequently, Taylor's view of regeneration focused on this faculty, for during conversion the heart becomes the graceful residence of the Holy Spirit which engenders there that foundation of all the affections, love. For Taylor this affection informs the response of the will to grace; it enables the heart to accept God's calling and to perform charitable acts, a notion which underlay both Taylor's meditations as well as the entire New England social experiment.

Etched in Edward Taylor's poetry are acts of the poet's will. In the *Preparatory Meditations* one discerns a will actively striving to turn away from itself and toward God, its proper object; for in the saint the converted heart evidences a filial love and obedience modeled after, albeit always less perfect than, that of Christ (C, p. 34). This love and obedience stem from the renewed power of the will to consent to the truth and wisdom revealed in Scripture and nature; and genuine consent to this revelation necessarily leads to the conformity of the saint's will to that of God. Searching for some indication of this saving attunement of his heart, Taylor wrote and preserved his private, diarylike meditations. In their focus on the will these poems reflect the quest of the poet's self for conversion, that is to say, for love and identity. If his will, the core of his whole being, were participating in the drama of regeneration, it would communicate some sign, perhaps in its external work, of its increasing conformity to God's will. Real self-identity lay in this loving adherence and conformity.[66] However, since regeneration is progressive, one's

66. Roy Harvey Pearce, failing to take into consideration exactly what the will meant to Taylor, concludes that "even in the best of Taylor's poetry the value put on specifically human experience is minimal" and that "it is the meaning of the God ordered world, of God himself, which is important, not the fact that a man faces that meaning" ("Edward Taylor: The Poet as Puritan," *New England Quarterly*, 23, March 1950, 43). In

perception of his love, that is, his insight into the quality of his will's response to God's design, must be equally continuous and developing. Taylor thus strove to maintain a passive and an active disposition in his heart—"Will thy Will, I must" (1.16, 11)—offered to God in love: "Make mee thy Lunar Body to be filld / In full Conjunction, with thy Shining Selfe" (2.21, 31–33). He devotedly sought a "new Moon day" when he would no longer be eclipsed by sin, when he would discover his complete identity. Then his attuned will would, especially through loving poetic song, reflect back to God His own love.

---

contrast, Michael Colacurcio perceives in *Gods Determinations* Taylor's "sense of addressing real people in a concrete historical situation" (*"Gods Determinations Touching Half-Way Membership:* Occasion and Audience in Edward Taylor," p. 299).

Part Two: Word

Chapter IV

Nonsense from a Lisping Child

The Word as Piety

Understanding Taylor's poetry also requires a consideration of his Christology, for he held Christ to be the primary subject and the ultimate object of true verse. However, since in most respects Taylor's theological notions of Christ are orthodox, it is necessary to emphasize only those aspects of his christological thought which are germane to his conception of the human will. Such a review provides evidence that both psychological notions derived from the Renaissance idea of the soul's faculties and christological beliefs inherited from the church fathers, especially from Augustine, underlie Taylor's thought on language.

Taylor perceived, first of all, an analogy between the Trinity and man's mind (Father), with its reason (Son) and will (Holy Spirit). In this scheme words, which are conceived in the will or heart, are intimately related to the Logos, or Word. Second, in accord with conventional Puritan thought, Taylor stressed the role of language in conversion. From his poetic perspective he saw words as the foremost mode of practical piety. For him the

93

use of words in thought, writing, and speech was a sacred duty encompassing all other exercises of the will. In fact, he interpreted each of the will's modes of expression—those of thought, word, and deed—as fundamentally a verbal response to God. Each of these responses, but especially words, reflects a man's self and thereby serves as an index to the spiritual condition of his entire being.

Recognition of these matters reveals that although, as far as we know, Taylor never formulated a systematic theory of language, he nonetheless maintained a number of related concepts of the word.[1] It follows that because these ideas are embodied in his art, they are important to our appreciation of Taylor's current status as the most remarkable poet to emerge from Puritan New England.

i

In patristic thought, at least from the time of Justin Martyr, the Son of God has been traditionally associated with the Logos, the Word of the Father. Derived from the mind of and spoken by the Father, the Word reflects God's eternal idea, particularly his wisdom.[2] It is to the Son, consequently, that Taylor and other Puritans directed the faculty of reason in their quest for truth; for the Son, as "All Wisdoms Fulness" (1.27, 20), incorporates the Father's intellect.

More central to Taylor's thought is the Word's embodiment of the other power of the Father's mind, namely his will. The will of the Father and of the Son is one and inseparable; from the very beginning the Son covenanted to do the will of the Father.[3] Thus Christ, as the Word made flesh, bears "the Counsill" of

1. Recent studies which describe aspects of Taylor's view of writing are: Carlisle, "The Puritan Structure of Edward Taylor's Poetry"; Donald A. Junkins, " 'Should Stars Wooe Lobster Claws?': A Study of Edward Taylor's Poetic Practice and Theory," *Early American Literature*, 3 (Fall 1968), 88–117; and Mignon, "Edward Taylor's *Preparatory Meditations:* A Decorum of Imperfection."

2. See *Edwards on the Trinity*, pp. 89–90.

3. See Augustine, *The Trinity*, 2.5.9; Reynolds, *A Treatise of the Passions*, p. 83; Willard, *Compleat Body*, pp. 13, 563.

the divine will and is designated to communicate to man "the Whole Will of God" (C, pp. 113, 58; see also p. 124; 2.53, 25). His earthly will delighted in its conformity to that of God. The obedience stemming from this attuned heart was perfect in every respect (C, p. 272). Therefore, in conjunction with the quest of man's reason for truth, it is to the Son of God that one's will inclines in its search for goodness.

As we noted in chapter 3, however, the divine will was generally thought to be manifested by the Holy Spirit. This matter raises no real problem because God bestowed the Spirit upon the Son and upholds him by it; the Son's entire being is imbued with the Spirit.[4] Consequently, since the Father desires the influence of the Spirit to be spread through the Word, it is Christ who confers on man the graces of the Holy Ghost (TCLS, pp. 136, 169; C, p. 59; 2.91, 30). This union of the Spirit and the Word is depicted by Taylor in two passages referring to Christ's eyes. In the prose statement Taylor explicitly writes that, "Christs eye was influenced by Gods Will" (C, p. 465); in the meditation he poetically attributes "Dove like Eyes" (2.119, 3) to Christ. Since the dove is the traditional Christian symbol for the Spirit, which emanates from and manifests God's will, it is clear that Taylor is alluding to the indwelling of the Holy Spirit in Christ.

This union is further evinced in Taylor's association of Christ with love.[5] This representation is consistent with the tenets of Christian tradition (according to which the Holy Spirit betokens love or charity) as well as of faculty psychology (according to which the will engenders love). Thus, for Taylor, the Word or Logos is God's "rich Love Letter" to man, "Writ all in Love from top to toe" (2.8, 21, 23). The Son, infused with the Spirit and thereby manifesting God's will, possesses boundless Love (1.27, 37; 2.2, 25; 2.141, 43).

---

4. See Calvin, *Institutes*, 3.1.2; Edwards, *Freedom of the Will*, p. 281; Nuttall, *The Holy Spirit*, pp. 20-33.

5. See also Augustine, *The Trinity*, 4.9.12; Milton, *Paradise Lost*, 12: 402–4; and *Edwards on the Trinity*, p. 99.

He represents "a birth of Keyes t'unlock Loves Chest" (1.42, 5), "A Deity of Love Incorporate" (1.11, 1). Taylor's poetic theme of love is founded on this view of the Word.

Taylor, furthermore, saw the Word as the expression of the Father's Self. Insofar as he incorporates the Father's wisdom and his love, the Son manifests God's mind, that is, the composite aspect of his reason and will: "The Whole minde of God respecting all things is with him" (C, p. 59).[6] It is in fact owing to his relationship to God's mind or Self that the Son derives the title of Logos: "he is call'd the word, from the propheticall office that he attended . . . Christ being Conceived in the Fathers minde comes forth of the Fathers bosom, and declares what is the minde of the Father unto others" (C, p. 75). The Word, that is to say, originates from the power of the Father (mind) through the operation of the Spirit (will, heart, bosom) (C, p. 16).

As the expression of God's Self, the Word is central to everything. Since divine love, which the Son represents par excellence, pervades the universe (see chapter 1), "Christ lies as the Foundation of all" (C, p. 113). Taylor argued that "God hath gathered together all things in Christ (as their head) both of things in heaven, and of things in earth" (C, p. 301). This is so because all things were created through the Logos and because, subsequently, everything is sustained and governed by the Son (C, pp. 115, 121).[7] The Word endlessly communicates God's wisdom and love to all creation.

The Incarnation, as we noted in chapter 2, was a particularly dramatic occasion of this communication. It reasserted the Son's initial act of genesis in that God again conveyed his will or love through his Word, thereby revivifying created life. Christ's human form was made by the Father in the Holy Spirit (C, pp. 10, 48; TCLS, p. 206); his mission was to redeem man through the further divulgence and clarification of the divine will.

One of the reasons for Taylor's special artistic interest in the Incarnation lay in the fact that, together with its reassertion and

6. Augustine taught that the Son is "the Father's mind or intellect conscious of the Father's will" (*City of God*, 10.28).

7. See also Augustine, *The Trinity*, 1.6.12.

96

elevation of human dignity, it emphasized the mediatory nature of the Logos. It is through the Word's manifestation of God's inclination to communicate himself that eternity and time are essentially related. Taylor thus wrote in "The Reflexion":

> I saw thee Pearle-like stand
> 'Tween Heaven, and Earth where Heavens Bright glory all
> In streams fell on thee, as a floodgate and,
> Like Sun Beams through thee on the World to Fall.

The Word endlessly mediates from God to man (C, pp. 58, 292; TCLS, p. 208). However, whereas during creation the Word expressed an image of God, at the Incarnation the Word merged with that image. As a result of this personal union the mediation of the Word becomes more intimate:

> Godhead, and Manhood harmonize in thee.
> Hence thou alone wee mediator read,
> 'Tween God, and Man.
>
> (2.113, 44–46)

It is not surprising that Taylor depicted this most dramatic occasion of the Word's act of communication in literary terms. Taylor saw Christ as the "most Exact Coppy, written by the Deity of the Son of God, with the Pen of the Humanity, on the milk white Sheet of an Holy Life"; he referred to His life as "a Coppy written by the pen of perfect Manhood, in the Unerring hand of Godhead" (C, pp. 34, 102).

The Word is God's artist. He is the Father's hands in the act of creation. He serves as those creative fingers from which all designs originate and from which all life flows. Taylor thus referred to Adam as "The Daintiest Draught thy Pensill ever Drew: / The finest vessell, Lord, thy fingers fram'de" (1.30, 1–2).

The artistic achievement of the Word lies in his communication of the Father's will in divine love. Grace, the theological term for this love, is the Word's "sparkling Art Divine" (1.10, 18), which flows freely to the elect because the Word's "Tongue's tipt with sweet Heavenly Rhetorick" (2.128, 35). When Adam fell, sin *seemed* to banish this grace or love; nature, for instance, instead of phenomenally reflecting the poetry of the Word, took on the appearance of incompetent art: "Each twig is bow'd with loads of follies Rhime" (2.41, 10). But the Word's love or grace is unceasing and immutable; nothing can destroy or mar it. Sin actually accents the fact that everything remains in God's hands (1.31, 32). Even at the time of the Incarnation—that reassertion of creation—the Son did not refurbish the universe with love; rather, it was the occasion for him to "step in, and Graces Art improove" (2.75, 40). This improvement is primarily reflected in the saint's soul, where grace indelibly writes "in golden Letters" the Word's "Superscription in an Holy style" (1.6, 15–16).

All true art elicits a response, and the art of the Logos urges and enables the saint to conform to the divine will as well as to converse with God. The elect are to speak or pray to God through the Word, for owing to his hypostatic union of Godhead and manhood, Christ not only mediates between God and man but also provides the only means whereby man has access to God (1 Tim. 2: 5). Just as his manhood served as God's altar in the sacrificial redemption of man, Christ's Godhead is man's medium for offering praise to God (2.18, 23). The Word indeed serves as a two-way bridge.

Although he often drew attention to Christ's divine role as Redeemer and to his earthly role as exemplar, Taylor stressed the function of the Logos as mediator. Reflecting the Father's intellect and imbued with the Holy Spirit (will, love), the Word communicates to all creation an image of God's Self. Because his loving art of grace engenders all life, he is the foundation of and the key to the universe. The Word incessantly mediates between eternity and creation as well as between man and God. These christological notions informed Taylor's view of his own poetic art; for if the Father, speaking through the Logos, endlessly communicates his loving Self to man, then man, who is the most perfect and godlike of the creatures and who subsequent to the Incarnation shares in a personal relation to God, must strive to respond to the Word. He in turn is obliged to communicate himself to his Creator. For Taylor this duty requires the expression of pious words offered in love to God through the Word.

ii

Taylor accepted the concept that an analogy exists between the Father, Son, and Holy Spirit and the human trinity of mind, reason, and will. From this Renaissance idea, also found in the writings of Augustine,[8] he adopted the view that man's words are akin to the Word in origin and function. He believed that words are generated by the power of the entire mind or soul through the will in a manner similar to the propagation of the Word by the Father in the Holy Spirit (C, p. 75).[9]

Since man's words bear this analogous relation to the Word, they should express the thought of the soul rationally—"a word should ever carry reason in it" (TCLS, p. 61)—thereby imitating the Word's perfect reflection of the Father's idea. Language should be derived from "the Ore / Of Reasons mine," from "the finest twine of reason" (2.43, 7–8, 11).[10] Indeed, a lack of clarity in one's language signified the absence of the Spirit's illumination in the soul's eye. It was the fear that he had been denied this grace which goaded Taylor to bemoan frequently the inability of his thoughts to come to terms with God. His thoughts, though "the fairest Blossoms" of his mind, revealed a want of wisdom; "And so my words are simply ragged, nought" (2.141, 6–7).

The Logos, as we saw in the preceding section, not only mirrors the Father's intellect but also embodies his will or Spirit. Man's words, bearing reason, are likewise containers of will, for

8. See, for example, Augustine, *The Trinity*, 14.6.8. An excellent study of the literary implications of Christ as Logos is Kenneth Burke, *The Rhetoric of Religion: Studies in Logology*.

9. Increase Mather argues that "Words are the Birth of the mind" just as the Son of God is "eternally begotton by the infinite understanding of the Father reflecting upon his own glory before the world began" (*The Mystery of Christ*, pp. 76–77). In *A Mixture of Scholasticall Divinity*, of which Taylor owned a copy, Henry Jeanes compares the Son's revelation of "the *mysterious* Counsill of God" to the "*vocal word*" which "discloseth the mind of a man" (p. 66).

10. Reynolds called the tongue the "Messenger of Reason" and speech "the Gate of the Soule" (*A Treatise of the Passions*, pp. 505, 506).

99

the heart communicates its intent or inclination through the vehicle of language. This is what Taylor meant when he remarked that "Words are used onely to import the intent in the minde of the Speaker" (C, p. 273). For, though words always stem from the combined operation of reason and will (mind), they remain specially related to the faculty of volition. It is the will, like the Spirit in regard to the Logos, in which the word is conceived and by which it is given birth. Words "leape up" from the heart (2.106, 66; see also 1.48, 41–42; 2.17, 53–54; "The Experience," 25–28). Mental, written, or spoken words all originate in the heart, where they are first recorded (TCLS, p. 167; 2.19, 5).[11] Hence the true meaning of the syllables of any word lies in the will; a man's language incorporates and reflects the disposition of his will. Words indicate the moral condition of the heart.[12]

But one must be wary, lest he be deceived by what is spoken or written. Even the unregenerate, whose wills are indeed burdened with sin, can "tip their tongues with the language of Zion" (C, p. 392; cf. 2.109, 51).[13] To be sure, their expression is devoid of any real meaning in direct proportion to the lack of grace's influence in their hearts. It is, in fact, this very fear of verbal hypocrisy which Satan evokes in the elect of Taylor's *Gods Determinations*. Satan taunts them with the possibility that their prayers may in truth belie their secret thoughts and desires: "Thy Heart doth lip such Languague though thy Lip / Is loath to let such Languague open slip" (p. 425). Taylor realized that unless the will is predisposed to love God by the Spirit's grace, all pious words addressed to God remain meaningless. Such mental, written, or spoken words, even those of a minister, simply degenerate

11. See also Augustine, *On Christian Doctrine*, 1.13.12.

12. According to Increase Mather "words discover what men will and desire" (*The Mystery of Christ*, p. 77). Hooker likewise remarks that the "wickedness of the heart walks abroad in our words" (*The Application of Redemption*, p. 150). See Matt. 12: 35.

13. "Christ nowhere says, . . . ye shall know men by their talk, or ye shall know them by the good story they tell of their experiences, or ye shall know them by the manner and air of their speaking, and emphasis and pathos of expression, or by their speaking feelingly, or by making a very great show by abundance of talk" (Edwards, *Religious Affections*, p. 407).

into "a Magpies Chatter"; they deteriorate into mere "prittle pratle" (2.155, 29, 31). If these words are conceived in a heart which is the temple not of the Holy Spirit but of Satan, then the "Tongue's an Altar of forbidden Weare" (2.25, 14–15).

The dread that his will is not empowered by grace but is abandoned to Satan's whims and that, thus devoid of meaning, his heart will engender aborted, hypocritic words haunted Taylor:

> This Wracks my heart, and low my person layes
> And rowles mee in the dust at thoughts hereon.
> That thou, who dost deserve all glorious praise
> Should with an Empty Will, whose power is none
> Be paid, indeed; But yet, (O pardon mee)
> I want a power, not will to honour thee.
>
> (2.38, 13–18)

Taylor tried, as the last line suggests, to maintain both a passive and an active disposition of the will, hoping thereby to arrive at words the true meaning of which would testify either to the presence or to the absence of the Spirit in his heart. In order to achieve insight into his spiritual state, which passively depended upon God, Taylor shaped his heart's active verbal assertions of love into a collection of diarylike meditations.

That the Spirit dwell within the will is paramount. Although every man possesses the faculty of volition, only the elect can truly exercise it. As a result of conversion the saint's will becomes the repository of the Word's art; and the saint's ability to verbalize rightly depends on this act of grace conveyed by the Spirit. When the heart is transformed into the Spirit's instrument, the Word's art instructs the will how to tune graceful words of praise to God: "My heart thy Viall with this spicknard fill. / Perfumed praise to thee then breath it will" (2.62, 29–30). With the breath (Spirit) of the Word in his heart, man's "Palate Ulcerd Mouth, and Ill Tongue" (2.67 [B], 60) will begin to speak the language of the regenerate; then, explains Taylor punning on the word *say*, "My Sayles shall tune thee praise along this coast / If waft with Gailes breath'd by the Holy Ghost" (2.78, 47–48).

The verbal expression of Adam's will initially evidenced this effect of the Word's art, "otherwise it would not have been according to the Majesty of Infinite Wisdom, to have left with him the giving names to the Creatures" (C, pp. 208–9; see also 2.77, 7–12). But owing to the corruption of his faculties through sin, Adam and his descendants lost the ability to verbalize truth and wisdom. Words by the "Fall were spoild" (1.7, 14). It is, therefore, to Christ, as the Second Adam and as the Word incarnate, that the saint must turn, for He alone of all men since the Fall possessed a will in perfect conformity to that of the Father. In postlapsarian times only Christ's words, derived from his perfect will, embody absolute truth and wisdom; and it is he whom the saint is to imitate in "Holiness of Heart, and Conversation" (2.15, 38–40).

If the human will resembles the divine will in regard to self-expression, then in verbalization the heart's love must imitate the role of divine love. Man's love, the chief affection of the will, stimulates the generation of words by the mind in a manner similar to the function of divine love (Spirit, will) in the conception of the Word. Because the soul loves its reason and knows its love in the will, regenerate words, reflecting reason and first spoken in the heart, are conceived in and imbued with love.[14] Similar to the role of love in the Trinity, the will's love joins words to the mind; and it proceeds from the mind, in the will, through the word.

Taylor, therefore, felt free to interchange the terms *will, heart,* and *love* in order to designate the source of language; for just as God's will is his Spirit and his love, man's will performs by means of its love. The will's affections, of which love is the foundation, animate words (2.160, 2–3). Hence, though Taylor concluded that in his fallen state no "Pen and Inke can my hearts Love out line" (2.130, 6), he nevertheless faced the necessity of actively

14. "No one willingly does anything which he has not spoken previously in his heart. This word is conceived in love, whether it be the word of the creature or the word of the Creator" (Augustine, *The Trinity*, 9.7.12, 8.13).

exercising his will, in simulation of the divine will, in order that his "purest Love" might "sing" words of praise to God (2.116, 54). He understood that the quality of one's love determines the harmony or graciousness of the words conceived in the will. Were the loving artistry of the Word's grace to touch the poet's will still frostbitten by sin, then

> Thy rapid flames my Love enquicken will.
> Then I in Glories Tower thy Praise will sing
> On my Shoshanims tun'd on ev'ry String.
>
> (2.73, 52–54)

It is clear from the passages cited and from numerous others throughout his poems that Taylor perceived a close analogy between words and the Word. It is equally evident that this notion underlay and informed his celebration of the Word in sermonic prose and poetic song, manifestations of his vocation as minister and poet. Taylor firmly believed that God incessantly communicates himself through the Word and that man is not to stand mute in the midst of this expression of divine love.

iii

Besides the influence of faculty psychology and traditional Christology, Renaissance thought and Puritan literary theory also contributed to Taylor's view of language. Renaissance linguistic theory taught that perverse language signified a corrupted mind.[15] Taylor consequently believed, in keeping with orthodox literary theory, that logic is essential to proper verbalization; logical words reflect the uprightness of reason. However, since they are conceived in the will, words also necessarily evidence the heart's love. A proper literary style would therefore embrace both reason and will. This doubtless meant to Taylor that some degree of emotion should be conveyed in one's language, an idea not in conflict with general Puritan sentiment on verbal expression.

15. See T. McAlindon, "Language, Style, and Meaning in *Troilus and Cressida*," *PMLA*, 84 (January 1969), 30.

Puritans actually did not condemn the role of the affections in writing and speech. Rather, they merely contended that the literary expression of emotion, particularly in figurative language, should remain subordinate to logic and reason in the same manner as, say, the body was ordained to be subservient to the soul. At times, in fact, it is quite appropriate for the will to express its affections, especially in matters transcending the capability of the understanding:

> Reason, lie prison'd in this golden Chain.
>   Chain up thy tongue, and silent stand a while.
> Let this rich Love thy Love and heart obtain
>   To tend thy Lord in all admiring Style.
> Lord screw my faculties up to the Skill
>   And height of praise as answers thy good Will.
>
> (1.41, 37–42)

The Puritan relish for a plain style, therefore, did not require dry, tortured rhetoric devoid of emotional coloring. On the contrary, one's literary style should reflect the whole man, with reason presiding over but not choking off the affections.[16] In fact, since they are conceived in the will, words inevitably embody the whole man. Hence the more lucid are one's words, the more probable is the harmonious operation of his faculties. In this sense a plain style to some degree may represent, albeit inconclusively, the effects of the regenerative process in the author's soul.

This emphasis on style also arose from Puritan theological and psychological notions of the role of the minister's words in the drama of conversion, notions derived from various sources, not the least of which were those of Augustine. Sermons, Puritans maintained, were to be formally rational in content and in method, thereby providing, through the appeal of truth derived from Scripture, for the enlightenment of the understanding of the

---

16. Perry Miller explains that the Puritan "cry for a plain style and a simple manner was simply their protest against allowing the pill to become entirely sugar, against what they believed was the sophisticated practice of the great Anglican preachers, of covering doctrines with so heavy a coating of verbal confectionary that the bitter meanings were converted into a delightful seasoning for rhetorical gourmets" (*New England Mind*, 1: 304).

hearer or reader. The Puritan minister assumed the burden of responsibility. Unless his words bore truth, they deceived the mind (2.158, 4; TCLS, p. 160), particularly reason and will. The spoken words of the minister's sermon provide the key instrument in the Word's communication of grace: "the preaching of the Word is ordained for the converting of the soul to Christ. . . . The web of grace is wrought in the soul by the shuttles of the Word" (TCLS, pp. 40–41; see also pp. 5, 10, 71, 87, 158; C, p. 120).[17] Grace does not reside in the minister's words; rather, by means of the external syllables of the sermon the Logos internally affects the soul. Because they convey the work of the Spirit these words are indeed in some sense joined to the Word.

It is from the Word that the minister's converting words derive their meaning. That early Puritan divines rebuked their Anglican contemporaries for what they took to be an undue relish for words qua words is not surprising. Stressing their instrumentality as conveyers of divine intent, Puritan ministers doubtless agreed with Augustine that verbal sounds resemble the human body in terms of its agency, whereas the meaning of words is like the soul in regard to its superior relation to the flesh.[18] Though such an analogy is useful, we need to go beyond it in order to understand the Puritan view of words and their meaning. Since for them all language contains truth, words themselves are divinely inspired occurrences or events; this is especially so because before any word is thought, written, or spoken, its true meaning resides eternally in the Logos: "Words and their Sense within thy bounds are kept" (2.106, 15).

In order to communicate this fundamental meaning Puritan divines based their sermonic language on the two "books" of the Word: nature and Scripture. Because it manifests a more lucid revelation than does postlapsarian nature, the Bible, of course,

17. Willard remarks that although there is no "more *Intrinsecal Vertue* in *Preaching* than in *Reading*," there "is no small Privilege to *Hear* such, above the meer *Reading* of the Word; because they are enabled to Open the Scriptures to us, for the help of our Understanding them . . . and to urge the Arguments therein used, to move our Affections" (*Compleat Body*, p. 815). See also Cotton, *The Way of Life*, pp. 162–65.

18. Augustine, *Greatness of the Soul*, 32.66.

received more attention, though both were put to excellent poetic use. Like the Word itself, from whom it derives, the Bible is imbued with the Spirit; it communicates God's will to men through the "Spirits Pensill" (2.123 [B], 13; see also 2.79, 9). "Every Writer of Scripture was the Golden tongue, and Spirituall Pen" of the Word; "they were mooved by the Holy Ghost" (C, p. 395).[19]

It is quite natural, therefore, that Puritan sermons are generally framed by specific citations from Scripture. Since Puritans held that the minister's task is to win souls to Christ through language and that in the drama of conversion these words are intimately related to the Word, they further argued that the conversion of men could be achieved best through "the language of the faithful ministry of the gosple" (TCLS, pp. 18–19); that is, the Word's art, the grace of the Spirit, is best "introduced in the soul in the language of scripture" (TCLS, p. 42). As Taylor implied in his elegy on Samuel Hooker (1635–97), in order to be truly an agent of the Word's art, the minister must strive to familiarize himself with Holy Writ until, mirroring the running of grace from the creative hands of the Logos, "Scriptures [are] dropt even at his fingers end" (l. 80).

As with his sermons, nearly all of Taylor's meditations are also circumscribed by a specific reference to the Bible; for Scripture not only enlightens the reason which predominates in sermons, but, in the order of the rational soul, finally moves the will which especially pervades poetry.[20] The Bible provides "the golden Key" (2.115, 13) with which the love imprisoned in the heart can be freed. Taylor found in Scripture the art he sought to imitate— "Thy Word's my Rule" (2.126, 2)—and the "Golden Theame" (1.26, 7) he wished to celebrate in his poetry: "Make me, O Lord,

19. Augustine wrote: "Circumcise the lips of my mind and my mouth. Purify them of all rash speech and falsehood. Let your Scriptures be my chaste delight" (*Confessions*, 11.2).

20. However, to conclude with the anonymous author of "Poet in a Wilderness" (*Times Literary Supplement*, 60, February 3, 1961, 72) that "Taylor's imagination is utterly trapped in the Bible, and nothing exists unless it can have a biblical phrase attached to it" is to overstate the case. See also a letter by George L. Proctor (*Times Literary Supplement*, 60, February 17, 1961, 105).

thy Spining Wheele compleate. / Thy Holy Worde my Distaff
make for mee" ("Huswifery," ll. 1–2);

> Lord, let thy Glorious Excellencies flame
>   Fall through thy Gospells Looking Glass with might,
> Upon my frozen heart, and thaw the Same
>   And it inflame with flaming Love most Light
>   That in this flame my heart may ride to thee,
>   And sing thy Glories Praise in Glories glee.
>
> (2.128, 55–60)

As the expression of his heart, Taylor's poems are, similar to his
sermons, a "Superstructure" grounded on the "golden foundation" of the revealed words of the Logos (c, p. 268).

It is apparent from his sermons and poetry that Taylor's view
of language is consistent with Puritan literary theory,
particularly with its accent on the magnitude of words in the
experience of conversion and on the relation of these words to
Scripture. In the "Prologue" to the *Preparatory Meditations* Taylor
dedicated himself to "Write in Liquid Gold upon thy Name /
My Letters" (ll. 17–18). He realized that if he were truly guided
by Scripture and indeed devoted to the Word, his pen would be
rightly directed by the Word's art of grace; then his poems would
readily "Prove thou art, and that thou art the best" ("Prologue,"
l. 27). As the pun on *art* and the double entendre of self-depreca-
tion in this line imply, Taylor perceived an intimate relation
between his verbal art and that of the Word. Thus, in order to
imitate the Logos, he strove to base his words on Scripture; for
if his language were conceived in a will transformed into God's
"gospell golden mine of Grace" (2.155, 44), then his sermons
would become vehicles of God's grace to others. But equally
important, he would be able to assert his will and communicate
his whole self, through the Word, in poetic songs of love and
praise to God. This means that Taylor saw words not only from
a minister's standpoint (as instruments of conversion) but also
and more importantly from a very personal viewpoint: as the

embodiment of his own response to the converting art of the Logos.[21]

iv

To be sure, as we have previously noted, one's language provides no certain testimony to the soul's moral condition. Nevertheless, because he reflects or mirrors God's image and because he is the only creature endowed with the power to verbalize, man is inclined to communicate his will verbally in response to God's expression of his will and love through the Word. Moreover, if a man's heart has become the abode of the Holy Spirit, his whole being is disposed to converse about and with God. The saint's mouth should become "Christs Morter piece" which "lets granades fly / Of th'holy Ghost" (2.135, 17–18).

As a result of the Word's example and his relation to man, holy conversation is a sacred obligation. It is man's duty to express himself to God in affectionate words of prayer and praise.[22] Moreover, the creative Logos reflected the necessity of prayer in the two books of nature and Scripture. Man learns from his observation of nature, for instance, to ask:

> But shall the Bird sing forth thy Praise, and shall
> The little Bee present her thankfull Hum?
> But I who see thy shining Glory fall
> Before mine Eyes, stand Blockish, Dull, and Dumb?
> (1.22, 13–16)

Scripture, of course, makes the lesson of these natural types even more explicit.

Thus the elect, "inabled to draw out their renewed persons, and their renewing Graces into exercise" (c, p. 312), are obliged to praise God. For Taylor this exercise of the converted will primarily lies in pious words: "I fain would something say: /

21. See also Augustine, *The Trinity*, 15.11.20.

22. "God, although nothing worthy may be spoken of Him, has accepted the tribute of the human voice and willed us to take joy in praising Him with our words" (Augustine, *On Christian Doctrine*, 1.6.6). See also Willard, *Compleat Body*, p. 179; and James T. Callow, "Edward Taylor Obeys Saint Paul," *Early American Literature*, 4 (Winter 1970), 89–96.

Lest Silence should indict me" (1.21, 7–8). He feared divine judgment because his verbal piety may have fallen short of God's intention whereby the birdlike soul was "put in / This Wicker Cage (my Corps) to tweedle praise" (1.8, 7–8): "I am this Crumb of Dust which is design'd / To make my Pen unto thy Praise alone" ("Prologue," ll. 13–14).

As even the last passage implies, Taylor necessarily disparaged his verbal efforts. From the divine point of view nonsense is all a fallen man can offer in praise of or in conversation with God:

> Had I ten thousand times ten thousand hearts:
> And Every Heart ten thousand Tongues;
> To praise, I should but stut odd parts
> Of what to thee belongs.
>
> (GD, p. 418)

No words derived from a corrupted will can finally satisfy this duty (2.153, 17–18); literally and figuratively God "Surpasseth the superlative degree" (GD, p. 436). Caught between the innate impulse to express himself to God (2.38, 18) and the inability of his fallen nature to meet this duty, Taylor recorded in his meditations the utter perplexity brought on by this conflict. The following lines, the halting, clipped texture of which is organic to the poet's complaint, represent the epitome of the problem:

> My Phancys in a Maze, my thoughts agast,
> Words in an Extasy; my Telltale Tongue
> Is tonguetide, and my Lips are padlockt fast
> To see thy Kingly Glory in to throng.
> I can, yet cannot tell this Glory just,
> In Silence bury't, must not, yet I must.
>
> (1.17, 13–18)

Yet Taylor could not remain mute. In consort with the quest of reason for truth and the inclination of the will toward good, the word must, like the Logos, penetrate silence. Words, as containers of will, assert a man's self and project that self's search

109

for conversion, for meaning, love, and identity in the Word. Consquently, in spite of the fact that Taylor's "Muses garden thwarts the spring / Instead of Anthems, breatheth her ahone," still "duty raps upon her doore for Verse. / That makes her bleed a poem through her searce" (2.30, 3–6). Since he was obliged to communicate himself to God despite his sinful heart (the Spirit's garden), the poet resolved to meet this responsibility: "Yet being Chid, whether Consonant, or Mute, / I force my Tongue to tattle" (1.22, 21–22). To be sure, he concluded, even "Non-Sense very Pleasant is / To Parents, flowing from the Lisping Child" (1.34, 7–8). Maintaining what became for him a characteristic posture of a child before God, Taylor requested Christ to let each "unskilfull ditty still / Tunes in thine Eares, pipd through my sorry quill" until his poems of love stemmed from a will attuned by grace to the divine will (2.52, 34–36): "Accept this Lisp till I am glorifide" (1.43, 42).

v

The will, as was noted in chapter 3, responds in thought and deed as well as in word; that is, the will exercises the whole man. In Taylor's scheme each of these responses represents a mode of praise. He thus writes of the chosen that "In all their Acts, publick, and private, nay / And secret too, they praise impart" (GD, p. 459). Although sin infests thought, pervades discourse, and corrupts works (TCLS, p. 152), the merest touch of the saving grace of Christ—whose smallest thought, word, or deed dispels the enchantment of sin (2.56, 47–48)—empowers the saint to offer these expressions of the will to God.

Taylor understood thought or contemplation to be the articulation of the will in mental words.[23] Though these thoughts may never be outwardly uttered, they are "hatcht" in and are the

---

23. Augustine noted that "when our thought arrives at that which we know and is formed therefrom, it is our true word" (*The Trinity*, 15.16.25; also 15.27.50). In his essay on the Trinity, Edwards argues: "the outward word is speech whereby Ideas are outwardly expressed. The Inward word is thought or Idea it self"; "the Inward word is the Pattern or original of which the outward word . . . is the Copy" (*Edwards on the Trinity*, p. 91).

verbal response of the heart (2.99, 37). It was not unusual, therefore, for Taylor to link his inability to communicate to his failure
to engender adequate thoughts. Thought or mental words pre-
cede and inform written or spoken words:

> My tongue Wants Words to tell my thoughts, my Minde
> Wants thoughts to Comprehend thy Worth, alas!
> Thy Glory far Surmounts my thoughts, my thoughts
> Surmount my Words.
>
> (1.34, 3–6)

Just as with his notion of thought as mental words, Taylor
construed physical acts or deeds as verbal expressions of the will.
No one performs anything which he has not first thought or
spoken in his heart, the faculty from which every action arises.[24]
It is this idea of man's deeds as a mode of the heart's verbal
response which, among other things, informs Taylor's puns in
this line: "My handy Works, are Words, and Wordiness" (1.24,
28). Taylor is specifically referring, of course, to his vocation as
minister and poet. But, as we saw regarding vocations in the last
chapter, the work of a man's hands—whether as caretaker of
Christ's vineyard, author, or laborer—expresses that person's
whole being, for all action arises from the will. This view of work
is reflected in Taylor's ready use of images of labor to describe
his words, which are "but a Wooden toole" (2.23, 73), a
"Stack / Of Faggots" (1.48, 23–24), "packs of Sweetest Tunes
prest like a Carte / Loaded with cold hard iron, Sorrows layes"
(2.145, 3–4). In short, all deeds or acts constitute the external
manifestation of the word spoken in the heart.

Taylor understood thought, word, and deed to be equal modes
of the will's response to grace. Because of his view of the Logos

---

24. "There is nothing that we do through the members of our body, in our words and
actions, by which the conduct of men is approved or disapproved, that is not preceded
by the word that has been brought forth within us" (Augustine, *The Trinity*, 9.7.12). In
The City of God Augustine similarly joins acts and words when he comments on "the
marvellous nimbleness which has been given to the tongue and the hands, fitting them
to speak, and to write, and execute so many duties, and practice so many arts" (22.24).
"The heart of a man is the principall faculty of the soule, it rules all, it sets hand and
tongue, all within and all without a work" (Cotton, *The Way of Life*, p. 133).

as the expression of God's will and his own sense of special
vocation as minister and poet, he tended to refer to all the
exercises of the will as the language of the heart:

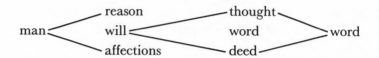

Thoughts and deeds are words. Together with words per se they
incorporate and reflect the whole man. With these concepts in
mind Taylor exhorted his parishioners to recognize that their
duty to communicate themselves to God applies to their actions
as well as to their words, that they should direct their whole
being in love and prayer to God: "Let your Lives be commentar-
ies upon the Commands of Christ" (C, p. 262). At the last judgment they would be taken to task for any failure to live their lives
in this manner. Then "All brought before him must be judged
by him, for all the things that are done by them, for Words every
one" (C, p. 63; see also 1.21, 8–10).[25] Thought, word, and deed
represent the gamut of response available to the heart. Since
each depends for its merit on the operation of grace's art in the
will (where Christ "turns the Scales" [C, p. 96]) and since each
is to imitate the Logos by communicating (through the correct
"Gam-Ut" [1.29, 36]) man's love to God, these three modes of
the will's verbal expression lie firmly rooted in the mediating
Word.

vi

Because the will is the focus of the Spirit's grace in the drama
of conversion, Taylor held that the word, conceived in and incorporating the heart's love, reflects the moral state of the soul.[26]

25. "All persons that have lived upon earth, shall appear before the tribunal of Christ,
to give an account of their thoughts, words, and deeds" (Westminster Confession, 33.1).
26. "There is no life in his words, if no life in his heart; and so for actions" (Cotton,

Though each man is to strive to perfect his will's verbal response to God, only the saint is actually capable of offering his thoughts, words, and deeds as a sacrifice to him. But the regenerative process remains incomplete in his temporal life, and even the saint is often plagued by the fear that his "Lumpish Heart" will fail to "Ascend the golden Ladder of [God's] praise" (2.145, 1–2). The key lies, of course, in the final effect of the Word's art; for only in heaven will the saint's heart, perfected by grace, evidence the unqualified obedience requisite to consummate practical piety. In other words, his entire being must be in complete harmony if the saint is to manifest true piety in thought, word, and deed. Then he can say, "My Faculties all deckt with grace shall Chime / Thy praise" (2.107, 59–60). In heaven his soul, that center of his whole being, will be transformed into what it originally was, "a glorious Musicall Instrument" which the Holy Spirit has "strung . . . with the golden Wyer of Grace & heavenly Glory, having screw'd up the strings to sound forth the songs of Zions King; the pouring forth of the Influence of Glory play upon the Soule Eternall praises unto God."[27]

Nevertheless, while in this world, the saint is to seek this harmony through the conformity of his will to that of God as revealed by Christ or the Logos, for all true obedience is "rightly hindg'd / Lord on thy word" (2.94, 21–22). If the words Taylor wrote or spoke were framed by Scripture, they might mirror this conformity, this regenerating work of the Spirit in his heart. Because he believed that "Words and their Sense within [Christ's] bounds are kept," Taylor saw the Word as the foundation of everything. Thus his own artistry, his verbal "Superstructure," must cling to, echo, and imitate the Word.

It follows that since they are containers of will, words reflect one's self. They represent the whole man in the same way as the Word expresses the divine Self to man. It was the quest for this self-identity that moved Taylor to keep a record of the verbal response of his heart. In his thoughts, words, and works—but

---

The Way of Life, p. 214).
27. Westfield "Church Record," p. 66.

particularly in his poetic words—he strove to discern a clue to
the moral state of his soul and to offer his whole being, his whole
self, to God through the love of his heart. He hoped to reflect an
image of the Word in his verbal piety, to catch a glimpse of the
Word's art mirrored in his own words. Only the "sweetning heart
breath" (2.126, 36) of the Word could transform the artless
verbal nonsense of the poet's lisping will into a similar "Oderif'-
rous breath," which "twisted in my Tunes, thy praise shall
ring / On my Shoshannim's sweetest Well tun'de string" (2.69,
40–42).

Part Three: Poet

Chapter V

Tending the Lord
in All Admiring Style

The Poetic Word

Numerous exclamations of self-disparagement abound in Taylor's poetry: "My blottings Jar / And wrack my Rhymes to pieces" (1.10, 31–32); "my inke is dim, / My pensill blunt" (2.7, 4–5); "Speech is too Course a web for me to cloath / My Love to thee in or it to array" (2.146, 2–3). These are so frequent, in fact, that they nearly constitute an underlying theme. But such complaints should not be interpreted to refer only to Taylor's personal sense of incompetence as a poet; rather they also represent his recognition of the inability of any man to derive merit from the exercise of his will in thought, word, or deed. He makes this same point in the concluding paragraph of the *Christographia:* "all our pensills in all their draughts attain not to anything of the Excellancies of Christ's operations. Ours are Worth nothing without he puts the Worthiness of his on them" (p. 468). Taylor was admonishing his parishioners and reminding himself of the folly of educing any sense of spiritual security from the apparent meritoriousness of the will's acts of piety.

117

Damning presumption may lurk in the feeling or conviction that one's thoughts, words, or actions betoken signs of salvation. Each man should, on the other hand, establish an humble frame of mind, suspending any sense of certitude concerning his spiritual condition. Humility dictates that everything be placed in Christ's hands, and this means, in terms of Taylor's vocation as poet and minister, that written and spoken words derive their merit wholly from their relation to the foundation and inspiration of all true art, namely the Word's web of grace (1.46, 31). Since grace surpasses all human artifice, Taylor naturally referred to his verse, comparatively speaking, as a "Dozie Beam" spun from the "Linsy-Wolsy Loom" of his will or self (1.26, 9–10).

However, if a soul were, as Taylor put it in one poem, converted into an alembic of the Word, then the will would become more capable of engendering loving words of praise to God (1.48, 27–30). These words, furthermore, would to some small but meaningful degree radiate that love and wisdom communicated by the Logos through grace. This is one of the principles informing Taylor's assertion that "the Wisdom of Divine Grace hath made the Old Serpents Wisdom a pen in the hands of his own Envy writing himselfe, whether he will or no, to be an Utter FOOLE" (C, pp. 24–25). Taylor is, to be sure, speaking in this passage of the limits of sin. But the positive implication of this statement lies in a logical deduction: if the Word's art operates even in Satan's perverse artistry, it must certainly be reflected in the words or works of the saint's will. Whereas sin temporarily "blurd" the divine "Print" or the image of God's loveliness in the soul, grace, by initiating the regenerative process, effects a partial restoration. This reassertion of the divine imprint by the Word's artistry is necessarily mirrored in the exercise of the saint's whole being, in both the internal and external language of the heart (2.8, 37–42). For the elect, it is through the Word's art that

> That Golden Mint of Words, thy Mouth Divine,
> Doth tip these Words, which by my Fall were spoild;

> And Dub with Gold dug out of Graces mine
> That they thine Image might have in them foild.
>
> (1.7, 13–16)

For Taylor all true art is modelled after and totally dependent upon the Word; and such art can be derived solely from the hearts of the elect.

The heart or will is, as we have seen, at the center of the *Preparatory Meditations*. Taylor turned to poetry because it was private and allowed him to concentrate less on the logic of the understanding and more on the affections of the heart. In poetry, we might speculate, he found release from the confining discipline of public sermons; but at the very least it doubtless provided him with an opportunity to delve into the question of his own salvation. As the *Preparatory Meditations* makes evident, Taylor's pent-up, heartfelt feelings tended to overflow all restraining rhetorical structures, even occasionally that of meter and rhyme.

Of course Taylor never abandoned reason in his poetry. As we saw in the last chapter, rationality comprises part of the inherent nature of words. Furthermore, the poet did exercise rational restraint, perhaps in imitation of the underlying rational order of the Word's poetic genesis of the universe, through the discipline of stanzaic form, meter, and rhyme.

Nevertheless, it was for its capacity to convey his deep love of God that Taylor wrote poetry. In this mode of expression he sought "To tend [the] Lord in all admiring Style" (1.41, 39–40), a style which, hopefully arising from a heart responding to grace, would communicate his love. Because the "Magnificence of the Authour is blazond by his Works" (c, p. 466.), Taylor looked to the expression of self in his pious poetry for some reflection, however obscure, of the spiritual condition of his soul. Without grace the "Quaint Metaphors" and "Sparkling Eloquence" of his poetic devotion to God indeed "would appeare as dawbing pearls with mud" (1.13, 1–4). But were he animated by the Word's art, he would more readily approximate, though never fully achieve in this world, a poetic style mirroring this Love—an "all admiring Style." Then his poetry, no longer "dawbing

119

pearls with mud," would imitate the artistry of the Word: "An heap of Pearls is precious: but they shall / When set by Art Excell" (GD, p. 456).

Thus Taylor turned to meditative poetry in order to record the inward drama of his quest for conversion. He saw poetic expression as the worthiest, most excellent form of literary devotion he could offer God, as the most persuasive way he could actively dispose his will to a passive reliance on God, and as the best means of catching glimpses of his own spiritual state. As the preceding chapters have argued, an assessment of the aesthetic achievement of this poetry must take into consideration his psychological and theological tenets. In this light this chapter will discuss the following four concerns: (1) how Taylor's view of the will and words informed the structure of the poems in the *Preparatory Meditations;* (2) how his concept of the Word led to the images of meditation which he frequently associated with language; (3) how his notion of words influenced and determined his poetic style and diction; and (4) how each of these points related to his use of metaphor, to the two primary sources of his imagery: nature and human activity, and to circular imagery in particular. An understanding of these matters will, hopefully, yield insight into Taylor's craft, providing at the same time a foundation for the discussion of his alleged mysticism in the following chapter. By means of this approach we can attain a better appreciation of the uniqueness of Taylor's art and of the merits of his poetic achievement.

i

The title he gave to the poems apparently written in relation to his celebration of the Lord's Supper suggests that Taylor may have intentionally structured them according to the prevalent meditative conventions of his time. He could have learned these practices in England, where he lived until the age of twenty-five or twenty-six (1668) and where an influential Puritan treatise on meditation, Richard Baxter's *The*

Saints Everlasting Rest, was published in 1650.[1] This work enjoyed an outstanding reputation in England during the second half of the seventeenth century and became well known in New England. Baxter was in fact an acquaintance of Increase Mather.[2] A reading of Baxter's work impresses upon the student of Taylor's verse how suitable the meditative structure must have been for the poet. It provided him with an apt framework for the poetic expression of his focus on the will, his concentration on the theme of love, and his concern with verbal piety. Thanks to Louis Martz's excellent analysis of the subject, it will not be necessary for me to detail the meditative conventions of the seventeenth century. It is valuable, however, to comment on how the general meditative pattern was appropriate to Taylor's notions of the will and its words and, as well, on how it thereby suited his poetry.

The traditional meditation involved an awareness of the faculties of the soul, which Martz distinguishes as memory, understanding, and will. In the meditative scheme the mind or memory first establishes the topic to be contemplated, reason then analyzes it, and finally the will responds to it affectionately. Of Taylor's poems, such meditations as 2.36 and 2.48 tend to follow this tripartite sequence.[3] Yet it is fair to say that Taylor did not rigidly conform to this pattern. This is not to imply that the emphasis of the meditative tradition on the faculties is not equally prominent in Taylor's verse. The poet was, I believe, less

---

1. Martz, *The Poetry of Meditation*, p. 154. See also his foreword to *The Poems of Edward Taylor*, p. xxiv. Although Taylor's library did not contain a copy of *The Saints Everlasting Rest*, it did have, according to Thomas H. Johnson (*The Poetical Works of Edward Taylor*, p. 207, no. 38; p. 211, no. 83), two other works by Baxter: *A Key for Catholicks to open the jugling of the Jesuits* (1659), and *The True and only way of concord of all the Christian churches* (1680).

2. Kenneth B. Murdock, *Increase Mather, the Foremost American Puritan*, pp. 266–67. Taylor spent at least two nights in Mather's home and was later influenced by Mather to accept the call to Westfield. They apparently corresponded: see "Edward Taylor to Increase Mather," *Collections of the Massachusetts Historical Society*, 4th ser., 8 (1868), 629–31.

3. In *The Meditative Poem: An Anthology of Seventeenth-Century Verse* (pp. 485–517), editor Louis Martz has collected several of Taylor's poems which he believes conform to this pattern.

interested in the formal process of meditation than in its fulfillment: "the exercise of our Memory and Understanding in Meditation, is ordained to the motion of our will."[4] Taylor most
likely adopted and adapted the meditative system because, in
regard to his concern with the psychology of the will, it furnished
him with a ready means whereby he could actively manifest the
verbal piety of his heart and simultaneously keep a record of its
progress.

Moreover, it is evident that the meditative structure permitted
the poet to dwell on the theme of love. Since this system of
personal piety was to elicit the movement of the will, it was
necessarily suited to the expression of love,[5] the heart's chief
affection. In fact, according to the Salesian spirit of meditation,
which differs from the Jesuit spirit in degree of intellectuality
and emotional tumult, the language of pious contemplation was
to originate in the heart's love which it reflects.[6] It was meditation in this spirit which suited Taylor.

Taylor, however, modified the traditional meditative climax,
wherein by means of the aroused will, the entire soul "is lifted
up to speak with God in colloquy and to hear God speak to man
in turn."[7] In its entirety each poem of the *Preparatory Meditations*
represents Taylor's conversation with God, but nowhere in these
poems does God speak directly to the poet. Taylor believed that
God's communication to his elect is continuous and that, in
response to his grace, the very language of the saint's own heart
reflects the artistry of the Word; for, as we saw in the third
chapter, the will of the saint is the musical instrument God plays
in praise of himself. In short, Taylor looked to his own art for
a sign of God's voice to him. Thus many of his poems open with
a search for words to convey his heart's love to God and close
with loving words communicating the active desire of the poet's
will to be the passive recipient of grace. Mirrored somewhere in

4. Edward Dawson, "The Practical Methode of Meditation," in *The Meditative Poem*,
ed. Louis Martz, p. 13.
5. Baxter, *The Saints Everlasting Rest*, p. 301.
6. Martz, *The Poetry of Meditation*, pp. 145–47.
7. Ibid., p. 36.

that sequence is the presence or absence of the Word's voice or art; but nowhere in these meditations does the reader encounter any sense of comfort on the poet's part. Taylor could not be certain of God's communication to him, least of all in poetry which he feels is "dawbing pearls with mud."

The meditative pattern, therefore, with its emphasis on the will and love, provided Taylor with an adaptable framework for his poetry. Since it stems from and concerns the heart, meditation facilitates the expression of verbal piety. By means of these words of devotion Taylor hoped to unveil the imprint of God's saving communication—his love or grace—to him conveyed through the Word.

ii

Since the structure of his poems corresponds to his conception of the will and of words, it is fitting to consider Taylor's poetic language, especially as that language gained its special authority from the nature of meditation. Of importance in such a discussion is the issue of occasion. What time other than preparation for the Lord's Supper, the sacrament celebrating God's most awe-inspiring act of self-communication to man, would be more appropriate for the poet to express his whole being in love to God?[8] For the Saint—Taylor orthodoxly argued that only those thought to be probable members of the elect could receive this sacrament[9]—the ministration of the Lord's Supper is the time to assert his "vows of obedience afresh" (TCLS, p. 183). It provides an opportunity for him to assert his renewed self, to reexamine and give thanks for God's progressive attunement of his will to God's divine will.

This view of the sacrament contributed to Taylor's motives for writing poetry. Because he held that the accord of a man's will

8. A recent objection to the position that these poems are related to Taylor's administration of the Lord's Supper is expressed in Thomas M. Davis, "Edward Taylor's 'Occasional Meditations,'" *Early American Literature*, 5 (Winter 1971), 17–29.

9. See Perry Miller, "Solomon Stoddard, 1643–1729," *Harvard Theological Review*, 34 (October 1941), 277–320; and note 33 of chapter 1.

with that of God necessarily finds expression in the verbal exercise of the heart and because he believed that the commemoration of God's greatest act of communication required a special response from the saint, Taylor did not dare remain mute. He was certain that with grace he would be able to celebrate in his meditations the fundamental meaning of the ceremony of the Lord's Supper (2.109, 77–78); then he could rightly, meaningfully say, "this rich banquet makes me thus a Poet" (2.110, 24). Taylor hoped that his words would bear an image of the Word's art and thereby reassert the union of God and man in Christ.

This desire to give apt expression to Christ's union of God and man underlies Taylor's conscientious attitude toward his art. His meditations reveal the heart and hand of a genuine craftsman. As recent studies indicate, he carefully edited and revised his work, improving it through modifications of stanzas, lines, words, and sometimes even punctuation.[10] It is in this respect that Howard Blake's comment on Taylor's "painfully won speech" is particularly relevant: "Taylor's verse suggests the experience of a downright man brought to slow, careful speech won from the inarticulate meshes of his God-certainty."[11] Chief among the motivations for this conscious effort toward poetic excellence was Taylor's belief that since meaningful and pious words arise solely from a will imbued with grace, true literary art belongs to the regenerate alone. The more devout, the more perfect is the poet's verse, the more likely is the presence of the Holy Spirit in his heart. From this perspective an understanding of his use of words, style, and imagery is as essential to an appraisal of Taylor's poetry as it is to that of any modern poet.

Taylor perceived, as we noted in the last chapter, a real correspondence between words and the Word. Just as the Word mediates between God and man, man's words in response to

10. See Donald Junkins, "Edward Taylor's Revisions," *American Literature*, 37 (May 1965), 135–152; Charles W. Mignon, "Diction in Edward Taylor's 'Preparatory Meditations,'" *American Speech*, 41 (December 1966), 243–53; and Peter Thorpe, "Edward Taylor as Poet," *New England Quarterly*, 39 (September 1966), 356–72.

11. "Seventeenth Century Yankee," *Poetry*, 56 (June 1940), 167, 169.

grace can mediate, through the power of the Word, between man and God:

> Thou art my Medium to God, Thou art
> My Medium of Worship done to thee,
> And of Divine Communion, Sweet heart!
> Oh Heavenly intercourse!
>
> (2.20, 49–52)

When they are motivated by grace and when they reflect and are offered through Christ, in whom Godhead and manhood are eternally united, man's pious words provide a middle point at which, in a figurative sense, God and man meet in a medium of mutual love.

Taylor saw, in other words, the pious language of the heart as a verbal suspension between man and God. Words communicate the heart's love, and since thought and action are equivalent to language, words provide in a sense the *only* means whereby a man can express himself to God. Such verbal piety reasserts the union of Godhead and manhood in the Word. This view of words is clearly expressed in the first two stanzas of Meditation 2.35:

> My Blessed Lord, that Golden Linck that joyns
>   My Soule, and thee, outblossoms on't this Spruice
> Peart Pronown MY more spiritous than wines,
>   Rooted in Rich Relation, Graces Sluce.
>   This little Voice feasts mee with fatter Sweets
>   Than all the Stars that pave the Heavens Streets.
>
> It hands me All, my heart, and hand to thee
>   And up doth lodge them in thy persons Lodge
> And as a Golden bridg ore it to mee
>   Thee, and thine All to me, and never dodge.
>   In this small Ship a mutuall Intrest sayles
>   From Heaven and Earth, by th'holy Spirits gales.

By means of an unusual but highly significant argument, this meditation focuses on a single word: *my*. This pallid pronoun serves the poet as a "Golden bridg" and, by extension, as a "Golden Linck" between man and God. It reflects the union of Godhead and manhood in Christ because it is "Rooted in Rich Relation." The word *my* is neither a concrete image nor an abstraction; it is suspended between earth and heaven and it brings them together after the fashion of the Logos. As the second stanza indicates, this word and by implication all pious verbal expression of the converted heart are reciprocal. The act of communication travels both earthward through the Word's creative hand and heavenward through the loving poet's pen:

$$\text{God} \text{ ------ } \begin{matrix} \text{(Word)} \\ \textbf{MY} \\ \text{(word)} \end{matrix} \text{ ------ man}$$

If this word ("little Voice," "small Ship") is animated or blown by the "Spirits gales," then the poet's side of *my* must reflect the attunement of his will to the divine will, otherwise it would not be "Rooted in Rich Relation" and could not convey a "mutuall Intrest" of shared love. Though man is incapable of speaking to God if He does not take the initiative (notice that the word *heaven* precedes *earth* in line 12), once grace is received, the saint has the means and an obligation to converse with God. Taylor is explicit about this: love does not merely pass through the Word from God *to* man, but from heaven *and* earth. Hence Taylor wrote elsewhere: "Thine mine, mine Thine, a mutuall claim is made. / Mine, thine are Predicates unto us both" (2.79, 31–32).

These passages provide an analogue to a series of images in Taylor's verse which depict the Word and the saint's words as rooted in and as suspended between heaven and earth. Taylor also described this verbal bridge or link as a rail, for the Word frees men "from Sins Gulph each way, / He's both our Bridge, and Raile" (GD, p. 420). Words likewise serve as a pathway or pass linking the temporal and eternal realms; the Word, stretching from his heavenly "bright Throne" to man's earthly "Threshold" is the "Golden Path" which Taylor feared his

"Pensill" would never adequately imitate, trace, or "line" in words (1.8, 3–4). Similarly, Taylor complained: "Impossibilities blocke up my pass. / My tongue Wants Words" (1.34, 2–3; see also 1.3, 35).

Related to these images is Taylor's representation of the Word as a channel (1.32, 25–28; 1.37, 17; 2.37, 20–22), a gutter (1.10, 16; 1.32, 29–30; 2.126, 29–30), and a vein. The poet frequently requested Christ to "Ope to thy Blood a passage through my veans. / Let thy pure blood my impure blood refine" (2.1, 33–34). Such a commingling of blood would lead to a mutual sharing of the medium of love in the Word; and, consequently, with grace in his heart the poet would be enabled to conduct his verbal artistry to God through "True Loves Veane" (1.36, 72).

It was natural for Taylor also to use the image of a pipe to portray the mediatory relation of words to the Word. Since, in Taylor's thought, all language is founded in the Word, "The Golden Pipes of all Convayance ly" in Him (1.27, 31–32). His Love "Coms tumbling" incessantly to the elect, "Even as it were in golden pipes that spout / In Streams from heaven" (2.142, 32–34). Once the saint has benefited from this flow of grace, the Word becomes the means for a reciprocal exchange of love. Thus Taylor asserted that if God distilled His Spirit (love, will) through His "royall Pipe" or by His "Art" into his soul, then all of the poet's "pipes, were they ten thousand would / Drop Spirits of Love" for God (1.48, 27–30; 2.4, 27–28).

Taylor's use of the word *pipe* refers not only to a means of conduction but also to musical instruments and to the human windpipe, a play on words which readily reinforces his concept of verbal piety as a bridge to God. These latter two meanings and the entire motif of music to which they are related (see chapter 3) were Taylor's way of depicting the attunement of man's will to that of God. It is from this sanctified will that proper words or "pipes" arise. Indeed, just as Christ's mouth and "Winde pipe" conveyed "all Sweetness" from his heart, so the poet must seek in earnest to make his "Winde Pipe [God's] sweet praises sing" (2.126, 5–6, 54), a feat he can accomplish only when his heart has become the nest of the Holy Spirit, become attuned to the divine will: "That I thy glorious Praise may Trumpet right, / Be thou my Song, and make Lord, mee thy Pipe" (1.22, 23–24).

The role of the Word and of the saint's words implied by his pun on *pipe* is made more explicit in Taylor's handling of quill imagery. This motif depicts the dependence of the poet's verse on Christ's initial communication of grace: "Lord make me, though suckt through a straw or Quill, / Tast of the Rivers of thy joyes, some drop" (1.49, 25–26). With grace comes faith, the "golden Quill" that Taylor sought (2.82, 43–44); and by means of faith the Holy Spirit will make the poet's "hand its holy quill" (2.6, 5–6). In short, Taylor's quill imagery emphasizes the reciprocal exchange provided by the bridgelike function of the Logos and of words:

> Steep my Stubborn Quill
> In Zions Wine fat, mend my pen, and raise
> Thy right arms Vean, a drop of'ts blood distill
> Into mine inkhorn, make my paper tite
> That it mayn't blot. In Sacred Text I write.
>
> (2.58, 8–12)

It has been obvious throughout these passages that divine love or grace is the gift communicated by the Word. It is interesting to note further that just as he described creation as the flow of this love from God's hands (see chapter 1) and just as he represented sin as a retrogression or clogging of this fluid genesis (see chapter 3), Taylor appropriately portrayed conversion as the flow of the regenerating waters of grace into the soul. It is pertinent, as I noted previously, that the imagery of Taylor's first meditation focuses on this flow of grace. For Taylor, the Word's art is "the Whole Sea of Electing Grace, and Love" (C, p. 305). From the time of the "fluid" genesis of the world, the Word is "Heavens Golden Spout" ("The Return," l. 25), an "Holy Fountain" (2.26, 26), a "Living Spring," and "Graces Conduite Head" distilling "Heavens Aqua Vitae to us" (1.32, 27–28, 34).

Taylor thus turned to the Logos for the life-giving waters requisite to the conception of true verbal piety in his heart:

"Lord make thy lilly Lips to ope the Sluce / And drop thy Doctrine in my Soule, its juyce" (2.121, 17–18). Since Godhead and manhood are, to use Taylor's term, "run" together in Christ ("The Experience," 11–12), then if the poet were converted by the Word's art, his poetry would likewise be transformed: "'Twill turn my water into wine: and fill / My Harp with Songs my Masters joyes distill" (1.49, 29–30). Grace frees imprisoned love and thereby engenders a verbal fluidity in the poet. Whereas the language with which his "heart runs ore" now sounds a "dull note" (2.140, 3–4), with grace his heart would "breake forth in streams" of praise to God (1.40, 64). Then the elect, with whom Taylor hoped to be identified, "shall breath Sweetness in and out" to God (2.130, 41); "This gracious fulness thus runs to and fro / From thee to them: from them to thee again" (2.51, 31–32; see also C, p. 338). If "Rooted in Rich Relation," the piety constituting Taylor's part of the verbal conduit of love would inevitably reflect back to God, through the Word, an image of the divine artistry.

iii

This concept of verbal piety informed Taylor's poetic style. The homely quality which distinguishes his verse was a conscious outgrowth of his notion of the mediatory role of the will's verbalization. The frequent juxtaposition of quiet and harsh sounds, the vacillation between smooth and rough metrics, and the yoking of metaphysical abstractions to mundane images in his poetry were not unintentional. The apparent unseemly effect of such techniques and Taylor's self-disparagement or humble disavowal of his poetic skill should not lead us to conclude that he considered these qualities severe limitations which he was unable to overcome.[12] On the contrary, we must unmask the adept

12. Harold S. Jantz notes that Taylor's "genius lies in his remarkable ability to infuse abstract concepts, even theological dogmas, with the pulsating breath of life"; that in drawing his images "from every phase of daily and Sunday life," Taylor "rather prefers than scorns to use the most homely or plebeian image to embody the most exalted idea, and will even use an occasional vulgarism if it suits his purpose" (*The First Century of New*

poet behind the persona of "the Lisping Child." In fact, Taylor
gave us a clue to his deliberate manipulation of style in the
"Prologue," in which he asserted his intention to "hand a Pen
whose moysture doth guild ore / Eternall Glory with a glorious
glore" (ll. 5–6). The word *glore*, either the author's coinage or a
Scottish dialectal form of *glory*,[13] signifies Taylor's explicit design
to make his poetic style combine the grand and colloquial.

Taylor's style grew out of his christological, psychological, and
linguistic beliefs. Despite his protestation that it is "too hurden
a bearing blancket," Taylor's "homely Style" (2.141, 14–15) is,
I think, central to his art. First, it was an effort to present himself
as a child to God. This, as we saw in the last chapter, was a
characteristic posture for Taylor; for it is written in the Geneva
Bible that "Whosoever shal not receive the kingdom of God as
a little childe, he shal not entre therein" (Mark 10:15). But this
childlike docility and helplessness intimate more than the poet's
humble preparation for grace. It may, with typical Taylorian
ambiguity, also have suggested for the poet an image of the
possible renewal of his soul; for with grace the soul is made young
again, is transferred "out of Satans famaly, as a Childe into
[God's] own houshould," making it "a rightful heire of all the
Privilidges of his own Childe."[14]

Second, by juxtaposing the sublime and the ordinary Taylor
showed that the verbal piety of an inspired will reflects the whole
man, the unity of the soul and the body. Taylor stressed the
ordinary as well as the metaphysical because the drama of con-

---

England Verse, p. 81). Norman Grabo, maintaining that Taylor's roughness is occasionally
but not usually intentional, argues that the poet's self-derogatory comments represent
"more than a polite convention or a guise of humility," for "Taylor's roughness—part
of what modern readers call his metaphysical quality—is, in his own eyes, a fault, which
he attributes modestly to lack of ability" (*Edward Taylor*, pp. 104–5, 137). Donald Junkins
has argued well that "self-abasement in Taylor . . . is part of a larger methodology of
writing which is closely related to the Protestant worship service"(" 'Should Stars Wooe
Lobster Claws?': A Study of Edward Taylor's Poetic Practice and Theory," pp. 99,
104–16).

13. Johnson, *The Poetical Works of Edward Taylor*, p. 191 and Stanford, *The Poems of
Edward Taylor*, p. 531.

14. Westfield "Church Record," p. 51.

version affects the entire being of the saint. The will, as has already been argued, is actually a synecdoche for the whole man.

Third and most important, Taylor's poetic style was an outgrowth of his view of words. For him true verbal piety stems from enlightened perception and a response to the underlying rational design of creation, the harmonious integration of nature and eternity through divine love. If the poet succeeds in verbally reflecting this concord between heaven and earth, soul and body, he is giving testimony to the regenerating effects of grace within himself. Hence Taylor sought to make his expression of piety mediate, so to speak, between the temporal and eternal realms. Not only the poem as a whole but its very style was to embody and become a verbal suspension. By linking the earthly to the heavenly through sounds and imagery Taylor strove to imitate in his poetic style the union of manhood and Godhead in the Word.[15]

The following passage provides a simple, skeletal illustration of how this conception of style works:

> All Graces Fulness dwells in thee, from Whom
>   The Golden Pipes of all Convayance ly,
> Through which Grace to our Clayie Panchins Come.
>   (1.27, 31–33)

The thought of these lines moves from a colorless, imageless, hardly poetic statement concerning the abstraction of "Graces Fulness" to an image of pipes, which suggests the conduction or transference of grace to the temporal world; the temporal world, in contrast to the heavenly realm, is represented by two images, one sensuous ("Clayie") and the other homely ("Panchins"), as well as by the effect of the final cluster of consonantal and vowel sounds. The end-stopped line and its shift from trochaic to iambic metrical feet reinforce this movement.[16] Indeed, the transi-

15. Francis Murphy has remarked that for Taylor "the Word made flesh is the living embodiment of what art at its best can only approximate" (*The Diary of Edward Taylor*, p. 20).

16. Sometimes Taylor structured an entire poem on this movement. "Meditation 1.10," for example, opens with a description of grace as *Aqua Vitae* in the first two stanzas,

tions from vague to sharply defined images, the change from
distant to immediate objects, and the abrupt, even terse closing
of the verse technically match the thought the lines were meant
to convey.

More often than not, however, Taylor's poetic style resists this
sort of simple exegesis. The sequence of his thought does not
always move distinctly from the abstract to the concrete or from
the mundane to the sublime; usually there exists a more complex
amalgamation of the two. This may evidence a certain lack of
control on Taylor's part, but the reason probably lay in his view
of poetry as an emotional outlet, as an expression of the heart.
In this light his concept of poetic style would not have been
restrictive, limiting him to some basic, almost linear arrangement of thought.

Nevertheless, despite the emotional foundation of his verse,
the *Preparatory Meditations* manifests Taylor's conscious endeavor
to arrive at a style which gives a sense of fusing and of incorporating the divine and natural orders. Consider, for instance, the
following excerpts, in each of which the juxtaposition of a metaphysical idea and colloquial language or worldly imagery reveals
Taylor's effort to imitate or mirror the role of the Logos as well
as to incorporate the mediatory function of pious words in his
style:

> My thatcht old Cribb
> (Immortal Purss hung on a mortall Peg,)
> Wilt thou with fair'st array in heaven rig?
>
> (1.46, 2–4)

> Its mankind flowr'd, searst, kneaded up in Love
> To Manna in Gods moulding trough above.
>
> (2.34, 23–24)

---

refers to the passage of grace through the conduits of the Logos in the third stanza, and
concludes with four stanzas, each of which focuses on the depiction of the recipient of
this grace as a beaker, crystal glass, porringer, and beer bowl.

Thou Cabinet most Choice
Not scant to hold, not staind with cloudy geere
The Shining Sun of Wisdom bowling there.

(1.13, 10–12)

Teeth are for the eating of the Food made good
And meditation Chawing is the Cud.

(2.138, 41–42)

Christs works, as Divine Cookery, knead in
The Pasty Past, (his Flesh and Blood) most fine
Into Rich Fare, made with the rowling pin
His Diety did use.

(2.81, 25–28)

The images and sounds of this last passage, it bears repeating, stem from Taylor's intention to make the style itself reflect the meaning of the words it presents; for as we saw in chapter 4, it is *meaning* and not sound qua sound that matters to the Puritan. Both words and style, therefore, imitate the Word by mediating between as well as combining the divine and the earthly.

This aspect of Taylor's style is too recurrent to be dismissed as an inadvertent or undesired effect. It is true, to be sure, that the results of his technique may at times put the reader off; but it is important for us to recognize that this style is organically consistent with Taylor's notion of poetic language. The sense of impropriety we often feel was intended to underscore the majesty of God's communication to man through the Word as well as to convey, through an imitation of the Word's union of God and man, the poet's heartfelt appreciation. By focusing his attention on the mediatory role of his language, Taylor preserved himself from the snare of presumption (concentrating mystically on heavenly bliss) and from the pit of despair (centering solely on man's sinful condition). In fact, the more successful he was at asserting—explicitly in words and implicitly in style—the Word's marriage of the two realms, the more probable was his sainthood; for then his verbal piety would be mirroring back to God the Word's integrating art of love.

Taylor's idea of the mediatory nature of pious language and his fashioning of a homely poetic style are germane to his use of metaphor. Again the reader should not be deceived by the poet's frequent disclaimers. Taylor complained that his "Metaphors are but dull Tacklings tag'd / With ragged Non-Sense" (2.36, 31–32), that his "Quaintest Metaphors are ragged Stuff, / Making the Sun seem like a Mullipuff" (1.22, 5–6) because the Word's art surpasses the superlative degree of human achievement (GD, p. 436). "There are Some things," Taylor explains, "whose Excellency is flourisht over with Metaphors. We borrow the Excellency of other things to varnish over their Excellency withall. But Grace excells all Metaphors. The varnish laid upon it doth but darken, and not decorate it: its own Colours are too glorious to be made more glorious, by any Colour of Secular glory" (C, p. 253).[17]

Taylor warned himself, moreover, against an undue use of metaphor because an unchildlike display of overconfidence in literary ingenuity would signify a warping of his intentions and might smack of presumption. He was doubtless aware of the prevalent seventeenth-century sentiment that the creation of apt metaphors depended upon the right exercise of the faculties of the soul.[18] In Taylor's terms this meant that skill in metaphor was contingent on the operation of grace in his soul. Thus, though he employed metaphor to satisfy his obligation and desire to glorify God, Taylor always demeaned his ability to use it well: "I pardon Crave, lest my desire be Pride" (1.22, 7–9).

Yet Taylor never abjured metaphor. For him this figure of speech readily formed that verbal bridge to God and contributed to a style which was itself, as we have seen, a metaphor of sorts. Taylor's recognition of the value of metaphor predates the *Preparatory Meditations*. In a letter (July 8, 1674) to Elizabeth Fitch, who later became his first wife, Taylor reasoned that

17. This passage is central to Charles Mignon's interesting "Edward Taylor's *Preparatory Meditations:* A Decorum of Imperfection."

18. See, for example, Peacham, *The Garden of Eloquence,* pp. 3–4.

metaphor furnished the only suitable way he could relate his love for her and sense of union with her: "If I borrow the beams of Some Sparkling Metaphor to illustrate my Respects unto thyself by, for you having made my breast the Cabinet of your affections (as I yours mine), I know not how to offer a fitter comparison to Set out my Love by, than to Compare it to a Golden Ball of pure Fire rolling up and down my Breast, from which there flies now and then a Spark like a Glorious Beam from the Body of the Flaming Sun."[19] This view of metaphor as a mode of expression for the intimate bond of love between two people is further evidenced in one of Taylor's sermons. Explaining that "all Languages admit of Metaphoricall forms of Speech" and that "the Spirit of God abounds in this manner of Speech in the Scripture and did foreshew that Christ Should abound in this Sort of Speech," Taylor concluded: "this form of Speech is a truth Speaking form, Convaying the thoughts of the heart of the Speaker unto the hearers" (C, p. 273).[20]

Metaphor was for Taylor more than a mere rhetorical device. It permitted him to reflect in his poetry the underlying unity of the universe, in which everything demonstrates the "suitableness of one part unto another: and of one thing unto another" (TCLS, pp. 61–62).[21] This unifying force is, of course, the love which

19. William B. Goodman, "Edward Taylor Writes His Love," *New England Quarterly*, 27 (December 1954), 512–13.

20. Taylor's two most important authorities on the use of metaphor, as the above passages make clear, are Christ (see also TCLS, p. 17) and Scripture (see also C, pp. 39–40). He may also have been influenced by the orthodox Puritan understanding of the Lord's Supper, according to which the external signs of bread and wine are not, for the elect, separated from the spiritual meaning they signify (TCLS, p. 86; see also Kathleen Blake, "Edward Taylor's Protestant Poetic: Nontransubstantiating Metaphor," *American Literature*, 43, March 1971, 1–24). Moreover, such reputable Puritan divines as Thomas Godwin, Samuel Willard (see Mindele Black, "Edward Taylor: Heavens Sugar Cake," *New England Quarterly*, 29, June 1956, 159–81; Stephen Fender, "Edward Taylor and 'The Application of Redemption,'" *Modern Language Review*, 59, July 1964, 333) and Thomas Hooker (see John T. Frederick, "Literary Art in Thomas Hooker's *The Poor Doubting Christian*," *American Literature*, 40, March 1968, 1–8) may have reinforced Taylor's attitude toward literary devices. See also Kenneth R. Ball, "Rhetoric in Edward Taylor's *Preparatory Meditations*," *Early American Literature*, 4 (Winter 1970), 79–88.

21. Evan Prosser suggests that "in all his best Meditations, the tension between opposites is resolved by the flowing of one into the other. There is not metamorphosis

flows from the Word—that divine assertion and expression of God—who at every instant presents creation anew, infuses the world with grace, and mediates between mankind and the Father. The Word, as the Poet of poets, not only incessantly "gildest ore with sparkling Metaphors" his church and its members, the recipients of his art or grace (2.152, 7–8), but through his Incarnation became, in a sense, the supreme metaphor. In fact, Taylor's two references to Christ's humanity as a pen and to his Deity as the authorial hand (c, pp. 34, 102) imply the metaphoric view that at the time of the Incarnation his manhood was the vehicle and his Godhead the tenor. Hence, although a mediatory role between God and creation existed from the first, the Word provides, as a result of the Incarnation, a personal union, a vital and inseparable metaphoric joining of God and the saint cemented in mutual love.

It is not surprising, therefore, that the figure of speech which yokes the sublime and the ordinary is central to Taylor's verse. Since his words were to imitate the Word's mediation, metaphor naturally became his most appropriate poetic device. Taylor's use of metaphor, like his style, provided him a "small Ship," a way in which he could, in thanksgiving for God's personal union with man, send God his "Returns" (2.35, 11–13); that is, similar to its use in the letter to his fiancée, metaphor expresses his love, communicating it to God over a verbal suspension founded in the Word. To be sure, in Taylor's scheme the ability of a man to converse with God depends initially and finally on Christ's metaphoric mediation. It is fitting that Taylor, in celebration of the Incarnation and in imitation of the Word's eternal mediation, found in metaphor an appropriate way to communicate the language of his heart.

---

so much as there is reinterpretation, a process which reflects the basic wholeness of a universe in which all things need only be given their proper position to participate in the unity of the whole" ("Edward Taylor's Poetry," *New England Quarterly*, 40, September 1967, 388).

V

For the most part Taylor based his metaphors on images derived from nature and human activity, with the former largely influenced by Scripture. Both, in Taylor's view, bear a relation to the Word; when perceived rightly they reflect God's image. Consequently, he employed them in his poetic bridge to God.

Nature offered an obvious source of imagery. As we noted in chapter 1, Taylor held that nature, albeit giving an appearance of distortion after the Fall, remains the handiwork of the Logos: it is continually reasserted by the Word and imbued with divine love; it communicates the divine will, agrees with right reason, necessarily turns toward God's perfection, manifests within it a progressive hierarchy of glory, and participates in the order of grace. These notions, implying that no essential gap exists between nature and heaven, supported Taylor's use of nature imagery; for by doing so Taylor established his personal metaphoric bridge to God by way of the artistry of the Word.

The image of grace which nature bears is, of course, less perfect and less discernible than that manifested in Christ's works and words; His "Words are 'bellisht all / With brighter Beams, than e're the Sun let fall" (1.24, 11–12). Christ both excelled and improved the participation of creation in the order of grace. This is one of the reasons why Taylor's imagery tended to echo that of the Bible rather than to present a fresh look at nature; to the Puritan mind Scripture supersedes the book of nature. Nevertheless, neither his faithful dependence on Holy Writ nor the fact that postlapsarian nature obscurely reveals God's will discouraged Taylor from using nature imagery. Because it still reflects the excellency of its Creator as well as remains a noble instrument of the Word, creation evidences an artistry greater than anything fallen man can achieve. "Nature doth better work than Art"; in fact, man's every effort to create reveals art to be only "natures Ape" (2.56, 25, 43). It follows that since human art cannot avoid imitating the natural world and since that world is a vehicle of the Word's expression, nature truly represented a legitimate resource for Taylor's metaphors.[22]

Taylor maintained, furthermore, that God made the world for man's use. Each man was, as we saw in chapter 3, to exercise his vocation in terms of rightly utilizing the temporal dispensation. Simply put, God "Gave All to nothing Man indeed, whereby / Through nothing man all might him Glorify" (GD, p. 388); the "whole Creation doth bring all its Shining Glory, as a Sacrifice to be offerd up to God from, and upon the Altar of the Rationall Creature in Sparkling Songs of praise to God" (C, p. 312). This duty requires the poet, whose works are his words, to do likewise. Thus, in compliance with God's design, Taylor offered to God metaphors based on nature, the "Second Book," in a verbal bridge of praise and love.

In the following excerpt Taylor's imagery implies the place of nature as an instrument of revelation and, at the same time, functions as a metaphoric bridge between the temporal and divine orders:

> Christ's Spirit showers
> Down in his Word, and Sacraments
> Upon these Flowers
> The Clouds of Grace Divine Contents.
>
> (GD, p. 456)

Likewise, each of the following passages exemplifies the mediatory role of metaphors—two of which overtly echo the Bible— derived from garden imagery:

> Oh! that my Soul thy Garden were, that so
> Thy bowing Head root in my Heart, and poure
> Might of its Seeds, that they therein might grow.
>
> (1.5, 2–4)

> My Gracious Lord, I would thee glory doe:
> But finde my Garden over grown with weeds:
> My Soile is sandy; brambles o're it grow;

22. Norman Grabo makes some pertinent comments on the relationship between nature and language (*Edward Taylor*, p. 90).

My Stock is stunted; branch no good Fruits breeds.
My Garden weed: Fatten my Soile, and prune
My Stock, and make it with thy glory bloome.

                                        (2.4, 1–6)

Like to the Marigold, I blushing close
My golden blossoms when thy sun goes down:
Moist'ning my leaves with Dewy Sight, half frose
By the nocturnall Cold, that hoares my Crown.
Mine Apples ashes are in apple shells
And dirty too.

                                        (2.3, 1–6)

Taylor's description of words as fruits suggests that nature and language are related. Elsewhere he wrote: "Make each flower / Of Grace in me thy Praise perfum'd out poure" (2.11, 53–54; see also 2.126, 49–54). Taylor desired that his words be the distillation of "Zion's garden flowers" (2.35, 14–15) so that subsequently they might serve as "Slips" or cuttings used for propagation ("Prologue," l. 24). As these analogies imply, nature provides both God and man with a means of communication.

Taylor was, as an orthodox Puritan, cautious in his display of nature imagery. The artist, Taylor explained, needs to exercise skill in order to execute properly any literary device, especially that of metaphor (TCLS, p. 44). In Taylor's view, a preoccupation with verbal cleverness does not enhance the poet's effort to praise God. Such an excess, on the contrary, parodies the Word's art and ultimately points only toward a prideful will. Taylor, as a result, feared that without the guidance of grace he would inadvertently "bed [God's] Glory in a Cloudy Sky" and "besmeere [it] with Inke" (1.22, 10–12). Yet, even in this meditation his association of ink blots with a cloudy sky provides further evidence that metaphors based on nature were, if deftly handled, germane to his poetic expression to God.

The following quotation, to cite a final example, significantly demonstrates Taylor's view of the relation between language and nature:

My heart thy Praise, Will, tweedling Larklike tap.
My florid notes, like Tenderills of Vines
Twine round thy Praise, plants sprung in true Love's Mines.

(2.5, 40–42)

Here the vehicles suit the tenor. His association of poetic words
with birdsong and vinelike plants—the transition between which
is provided by the pun on *florid*—evidences Taylor's belief that,
since it reflects and communicates the Word's art to man, nature
represents a proper resource from which he could fashion his
metaphoric bridge to God.

Taylor turned less often to nature than to images of the instruments and products of human labor for his metaphors. The basis
for this usage lay partially in his training in Puritan literary
theory, which, at least in regard to the utilitarian aim of sermons,
advocated the use of illustrations drawn from daily human experience. It may also be traced to some extent to a recently identified Puritan meditative tradition, according to which "the gaze
of the meditator was assiduously turned to the real world. Experience, recapitulated in images for the stirring of the affections,
was seen as a limitless reservoir of inspiration."[23] Certainly
Taylor's concept of the beauty and sanctity of the right use of
earthly things inspired his use of these images. Moreover, Taylor
held that since the Incarnation the exercise of the saint's body
in some proper vocation may testify to the working of the Holy
Spirit in the soul,[24] in which case all such activity evinces a new
dignity; for the personal union of the saint and Christ resulting
from the Incarnation is both mystical and natural (C, p. 85).
Consequently, "our nature, as we are man Kinde, is the Same
with his Humane nature. And so he, and wee are united together
(*Genere*) in one and the Same common Nature" (C, p. 320).

This idea led Taylor to conclude that since God and man are

23. U. Milo Kaufmann, *The Pilgrim's Progress and Traditions in Puritan Meditation*, p. 174.

24. Kaufmann explains that the Puritan "stressed personal experience for several
reasons: he treasured it for its evidences of election, he appreciated it as a disclosure of
the kind of rational whole his life was elaborating, and he valued it as the private
tradition in which the authority of the Word was interpreted and translated into relevant
imperatives" (ibid., p. 205).

eternally united in Christ, the human nature of the elect must to some degree reflect divine qualities just as the divine nature of God must include human qualities.[25] When Christ converts or marries a man, a "mutuall power . . . results, as a Concomitant property thereof, unto the Married persons" (C, p. 409). Of course Taylor does not mean that as a result of the Incarnation the elect are in some sense deified; rather, he is referring to the fact that since they are blessed with grace, their whole being is in rapport with God's design. He further means that because of the Incarnation human nature in some way completes Christ. Though he is complemented by the elect only in his polity, still there exists a close relation in which "every Child of God shall in a Sort make to the Compleating of Christ" (C, pp. 307, 317).

In this light every exercise of the saint's will in thought, word, and deed to some degree partakes of Christ's efficacy and love, thereby contributing to the completion of His work. This concept, underscored by his belief in the sacredness of proper human labor and by his equation of work with words, informed Taylor's use of images derived from man's vocations and daily activities. For Taylor metaphors based on such images do not reduce or debase the divine but rather represent the elevation of all human endeavors as a result of grace, which endows the actions of the elect with Christ's efficacy. Hence Taylor applied images of human activity and labor in the verbal expression of his will to God. He saw his poetic self, for instance, as a loom and his words, typically equated to an implement of work, as twine, both to be employed by God in the manifestation of the Word's eternal web or design (1.26, 7–10; 2.74, 42; 2.94, 14–15).

The following passages demonstrate how Taylor manipulated metaphors based on the instruments and products of man's occupations:

> I'm but a Flesh and Blood bag: Oh! do thou
> Sill, Plate, Ridge, Rib, and Rafter me with Grace.
>
> (1.30, 27–28)

25. See Grabo, *Edward Taylor*, p. 99.

Oh! that my heart was made thy Golden Box
Full of Affections, and of Love Divine.

(1.24, 31–32)

Although I but an Earthen Vessell bee
Convay some of thy Fulness into mee.

(1.28, 11–12)

I'le Waggon Loads of Love, and Glory bring.

(1.38, 42)

Make me thy Chrystall Caske: those wines in't tun
That in the Rivers of thy joyes do run.

(1.49, 23–24)

Grant me thy Spectacles that I may see
To glorify aright thy glorious Selfe.

(2.155, 13–14)

Selected for its simple illustration of the bridgelike function of metaphor, each of these passages moves from the poet's world, through an image of work or its artifact (the artlike expression of the will), toward God. In each instance metaphor provides the link between man and God: between the flesh and grace, the heart and love, the body and divine fullness, the poet and glory, the poet and joy, the understanding and God's Self.

These quotations are admittedly elementary examples. Sometimes the movement from man to God is reversed: "Let Graces Golden Spade dig till the Spring / Of tears arise" ("The Reflexion," ll. 15–16). Most often Taylor abandoned this simple movement for the sake of a complex and interlocking series of metaphors:

Yet let my Titimouses Quill suck in
    Thy Graces milk Pails some small drop: or Cart
A Bit, or Splinter of some Ray, the wing
    Of Grace's sun sprindgd out, into my heart:
    To build there Wonders Chappell where thy Praise
    Shall be the Psalms sung forth in gracious layes.

(2.3, 31–36)

Oh! that this, Thine Authority was made
  A Golden Anvill: and my Contemplation
A Smiting Hammer: and my heart was laid
  Thereon, and hammerd up for emendation.

(2.53, 13–16)

It grieves mee, Lord, my Fancy's rusty; rub
  And brighten't on an Angells Rubstone sharp.
Furbish it with thy Spirits File: and dub
  It with a live Coale of thine Altars Spark
  Yea, with thy holly Oyle make thou it slick
  Till like a Flash of Lightning, it grow Quick.

(2.92, 1–6)

Make me, O Lord, thy Spining Wheele compleate.
  Thy Holy Worde my Distaff make for mee
Make mine Affections thy Swift Flyers neate
  And make my Soule thy holy Spoole to bee.
  My Conversation make to thy Reele
  And reele thy yarn thereon spun of thy Wheele.

("Huswifery," ll. 1–6)

Such illustrations abound in Taylor's verse. As we noted in re-
marking on the style of his verse, Taylor did not feel compelled
to delineate a simple or linear pattern for the movement of poetic
thought. His imagery of man's handiwork, like that derived from
nature, was informed *generally* by the concepts he held and, as a
result, was never restricted or limited in range or complexity.

It is evident, we might conclude, that in Taylor's thought
nature (reflecting the divine image and ordained for man's use)
and the elect's activity and handiwork (sharing in Christ's efficacy and equivalent to verbal artistry) provided appropriate
sources for his metaphors. He had, in fact, declared his intention
to look to nature and human activity in the final lines of the
"Prologue." Were he elected, Taylor wrote there, he would reflect the Word's art in his poetry; "then thy Works will shine as
flowers on Stems / Or as in Jewellary Shops, do jems." Taylor
is suggesting that creation (see the first stanza of the "Prologue")

143

and man's work or vocation (see the second stanza of the "Prologue") are legitimate resources from which he can create metaphors. These metaphors represent, in imitation of and in response to the Word, Taylor's verbal bridge of love to God.

vi

The use of these metaphors pertains to a related theme in Taylor's poetry: the saint's circular relation to God. The belief that nature points to God, that sin is privative rather than substantive, that love is the "mutuall Intrest" of man's heart and the divine will, and that the Logos and the saint's verbal piety reciprocally communicate suggest how everything progressively circles back to God. Taylor, in accord with his manipulation of music imagery (in which, as we saw in chapter 3, the saint and Christ alternate as musician and instrument), reflects this circularity in his verse. He similarly employs identical imagery in regard to the elect and to the Logos in order to emphasize the saint's personal relation to Christ as well as to convey the sense of the reciprocal and mediatory function of his own verbal piety, were it truly founded on grace.

Since the ability to express one's love to God stems from Christ's marriage of Godhead and manhood, Taylor depicted the saint's circular relation to God primarily in conjugal terms. A mutual power springs from Christ's marriage of a soul (C, p. 409). Thus the Church, that collective body of the saints, "fills Christ top full, because she is his Fulness, and indeed he fills her out of his all filling Fulness, that she might be his Fulness filling him again"; in other words, "there is in Christ, and in his Church a mutuall Inbeing" (C, pp. 300, 305). This is a motif running throughout Taylor's poetry.

> If thy Almightiness, and all my Mite
> United be in sacred Marriage knot,
> My Mite in thine: Mine thine Almighty Might.
> Then thine Almightiness my Mite hath got.
>
> (2.48, 37–40)

144

God's marriage or election of a saint engenders in his bridelike soul, with its partially renewed divine image, the capacity to mirror back verbally to God, through the Word, the love of his whole being: "The Bridsgrooms all the Brids, his all is hers" (2.133, 7).

This interchange, this mutual communication, is conveyed through the coalescing of various metaphors in Taylor's poetry. Cecilia Halbert has already ascertained the circularity of the tree of life imagery in Taylor's verse; she rightly observes, "God grafts into man, and man is implanted into God. God is a tree, as is man. Yet just as man is the whole tree, so is he the meanest part of the tree, a twig. Likewise, Christ as a man-God on earth becomes a mean twig, although Taylor is unable to achieve poetic balance in his use of the figure."[26] But this circular relationship includes numerous other images as well. Christ, for instance, is "the Pearle" (2.5, 6) and his elect are "Pearls in Puddles cover'd ore with mudd" (GD, p. 401).

Similarly Taylor's nature imagery, albeit primarily restricted to biblical allusion, depicts this circularity. Not only are Christ and the saint alternately gardens and vines, but both are each other's lily: "Lord make my Heart the Vally, and plant there / Thyselfe the Lillie there to grow"; "*Make mee thy Lilly, Lord and be thou mine.*" This implantation will result in the attunement of the poet's heart, transforming it into Christ's "Chrystall looking Glass / Shewing thy Lillies Face most cleare in mee"; "If thou my Lilly, I its Vally bee. / My Breath shall Lilly tunes sweet sing to thee" (2.132, 25–26, 43, 32–33, 53–54). The attunement of the will—the soul finds itself a "lilly made by Grace's Art" (2.131, 45)—is central to the poet's ability to mirror back in his verbal piety the Word's love. Taylor's heart must be reclaimed as "th' Vally where this Lilly grows" before he can proclaim in and through his art, "I am Thine, and thou art mine indeed. / Propriety is mutuall" (2.69, 37–39).

26. "Tree of Life Imagery in the Poetry of Edward Taylor," *American Literature*, 38 (March 1966), 34.

This reciprocal relationship is likewise evident in Taylor's use of metaphors drawn from human activity. Besides his numerous associations of man and Christ with box imagery (2.50, 47–48), he developed an unusual tenant-tenement metaphor:

> Thou'lt tent in mee, I dwell in thee shall here.
> For housing thou wilt pay mee rent in bliss:
> And I shall pay thee rent of Reverent fear
> For Quarters in thy house. Rent mutuall is.
> Thy tenent and thy teniment I bee.
> Thou Landlord art and Tenent too to mee.
>
> (2.24, 49–54)

Similarly Christ and the elect are both a cup or glass (1.28, 16; 1.49, 28) and alternately cabinets (1.13, 7; 1.25, 33). Again, Christ is "A Purse more glittering than Glory 'tselfe" (1.27, 16), in which the saint is "a Golden Angell" or coin (1.6, 12); with grace the poet mutually shares in Christ, and hence, "I Purse, and thou my Mony bee" (1.2, 29).

These and other circular images ultimately concern the heart, the focus of Taylor's poetry: "Lord make my heart thy bed, thy heart make mine. / Thy Love bed in my heart, bed mine in thine" (1.35, 47–48). Man's will, Taylor is saying, must first be in tune with the divine will before it can express itself to God through a verbal bridge of praise (2.126, 37–40), an observation which also explains the circularity involved in Taylor's use of music imagery throughout the *Preparatory Meditations*. It is the renewed divine image and a revivified love in the looking glass of the soul which are circularly reflected back to God in the musical or poetic language (thought, word, and deed) of the saint's heart. When the heart mirrors this divine image, the words conceived in this faculty will be "Rooted in Rich Relation." These graceful words, literally full of grace—"thy rich Grace doth tune my Song" (2.49, 41)—will imitate the Word's mediation of love: "When thou unto thy praise my heart shalt tune / My heart shall tune thy praise in sweetest fume" (2.145, 35–36).

Thus Taylor reasoned that were he elected by Christ, his response could be likened to a "Tenis Ball"; for were he thus "struck hard on th'ground," he would "back bounce with Shine / Of Praise" (2.142, 38–40). When in 1691 he wrote, "It needs must be, that giving handes receive / Again Receivers Hearts furld in Love" (1.42, 17–18), Taylor anticipated his later meditation on the word *my*, which, he would write, "hands me All, my heart, and hand to thee." When the Word's art, Christ's grace and love, is handed to the poet, the recipient will hand or "double back" this "Love with songs" (2.141, 46) comprising a verbal bridge of metaphor conceived in a renewed heart and based on the Word. Real communication, like the love Taylor believed to motivate it, is always finally circular.

vii

I have intentionally avoided the term *metaphysical* in describing Taylor's poetry, not because its style and manner in no way resemble that of English metaphysical poets, but because the label is, I think, too confining and reductive in an assessment of his achievement. To be sure, the unusual associations, the conceits, roughness, strained imagery, and literary allusions of his verse readily evidence the influence of those English poets. But poetic cleverness never occupied the forefront of Taylor's attention; and the critic who judges Taylor's poems from standards drawn from the works of the English metaphysical poets places the Puritan poet's achievement in a garish light.[27] One might, for example, easily conclude that "the trouble with some of his images . . . is not that the vehicle does not carry the tenor, but

27. "It would be a sad mistake to place Taylor among the great metaphysical poets; he does not have their eagle's flight nor ocean's surge, but on his own quieter, more domestic level his is genuine and of unquestioned quality" (Jantz, *The First Century of New England Verse*, pp. 81–82). Among those who have discussed the relation between Taylor's poetry and that of the English metaphysicals are Thomas H. Johnson, "Edward Taylor: A Puritan 'Sacred Poet,'" *New England Quarterly*, 10 (June 1937), 290–322; Wallace C. Brown, "Edward Taylor: An American 'Metaphysical,'" *American Literature*, 16 (November 1944), 186–97; Austin Warren, *Rage for Order*, pp. 1–18 and his introduction to the

that the vehicle is too great for the tenor, or, on other occasions, does not have the dignity of the tenor."[28]

Taylor's poetry can and should, nevertheless, be evaluated in the light of the criterion of decorum. The principle of decorum, the most significant one concerning the seventeenth-century English poets' use of language, required that poetic imagery and style suit the subject and intentions of the author.[29] In regard to his christological and psychological beliefs as well as in terms of his desire to reflect and imitate verbally the Word's mediatory role, Taylor's poetry generally satisfies the demands of decorum, a decorum as intensely private as the often archaic and idiomatically personal language Taylor used in his verse.[30] The poems of the *Preparatory Meditations*, as the preceding discussion has argued, are appropriate to Taylor's poetic objective of expressing his love to God.

As we have already noted the recognition of this poetic purpose does not necessarily imply that Taylor was always in control. There are occasional excesses in imagery and diction which are beyond exoneration. On the other hand, an awareness of his intentions provides a key to the decorum of his verse and a means whereby we can perceive the uniqueness of Taylor's poetry as well as the manner, which reflects New England Puritan traditions. His psychological notions of the will and of language, his theological concepts of the Logos, as well as his view of nature and human work shaped his effort to reflect the Word's art in the verbal response of his heart. He thus sought to fashion

---

Taylor selections in *Major Writers of America*, ed. Perry Miller, 1: 51–62; Herbert Blau, "Heaven's Sugar Cake: Theology and Imagery in the Poetry of Edward Taylor," *New England Quarterly*, 26 (September 1953), 337–60; Black, "Edward Taylor: Heavens Sugar Cake," pp. 159–81; Emma L. Shepherd, "The Metaphysical Conceit in the Poetry of Edward Taylor (1644?–1729)," Diss. University of North Carolina, 1960; Martz, "Foreword," *The Poems of Edward Taylor*, pp. xiii–xxxvii; Martha Ballinger, "The Metaphysical Echo," *English Studies in Africa*, 8 (March 1965), 71–80; and Hyatt H. Waggoner, "Edward Taylor," *American Poets: From the Puritans to the Present*, pp. 16–17.

28. Blau, "Heaven's Sugar Cake," p. 359.

29. See Tuve, *Elizabethan and Metaphysical Imagery*, p. 192.

30. See Mignon, "Diction in Edward Taylor's 'Preparatory Meditations,' " pp. 243–53 and Karl Keller, "The Example of Edward Taylor," *Early American Literature*, 4 (Winter 1970), 11–12.

suitable metaphors derived from images of nature and human activity as well as to create a style which yoked the grand to the colloquial in order to embody his will's loving response to the divine love manifested in Christ's union of Godhead and manhood—precisely what is celebrated by the Lord's Supper, the occasion designated by the title Taylor gave his meditations. His poetic decorum is mimetic: just as the Word mediates between God and man, Taylor's poetry, offered in imitation of and through the Word, represents his personal bridge to God. This, and not the recognition of the *contemptus mundi* theme, explains why one may conclude that in Taylor's poetry there is "relatively little of that tension between attachment to things temporal and longing for things eternal."[31]

It was through the poetic expression of his Puritan beliefs that Taylor, poet of Christ, endeavored to tend his Lord "in all admiring Style." In his ability to manifest his poetic aims, especially in the realization of a stylistic integration of the sublime and the ordinary, lay the evidence of his salvation. Since words are derived from the will, a converted heart will spawn a certain degree of gracious verbal eloquence based not on superficial rhetoric but on the radical meaning beneath all rhetoric, on the integrating presence of divine love both in the soul and in the world. It is Taylor's effort to discern the spiritual state of his will through the looking glass of his poetic stuttering which informs the dramatic sense of anxiety we feel in his meditations; for the words themselves are events, uncertain events which motivated Taylor, in spite of his unrelenting effort to express his love in pious poetry, to keep the question of his spiritual condition suspended. He never permitted himself to cross the verbal bridge of his meditations in order to arrive at complete spiritual resolution or mystical assurance.

31. Waggoner, "Edward Taylor," p. 17.

CHAPTER VI

Man's Wildred State and the Curious Needlework of Providence

THE POETIC SELF

Edward Taylor's verbal piety stemmed from an aroused sense of poetic self. His poetry, especially the *Preparatory Meditations*, represents the assertion of this self in quest for divine love, for that true identity which informs all creation and which, in terms of human regeneration, proceeds from grace in the experience of conversion. Hence, throughout his poetry the will, the faculty primarily associated with the self, necessarily remains distinct and prominent. This means, among other things, that although voluntarily dedicated to serve Christ in every way, Taylor's will was never lost in mystical union with the divine will. As the numerous images of human activity in his poetry suggest, the poet's self, like the expression stemming from it, was firmly rooted in the temporal world. Recognizing that all men live in an experiential context—even Christ was tutored by earthly experience (2.41, 35–36)—Taylor, in the dual but related vocations of poet and minister, conducted his search for self-identity within the vicissitudes of time. As a Christian pilgrim he did not seek

150

escape from the divinely decreed progress of life's trials. Rather, in accordance with the design of Providence, he sought to ferret out of his "Wildred state" and the apparent "Crooked Passages" of his daily existence the essential meaning of his real identity either as a loving child of God or as a degenerate heir to hell (GD, p. 449). His was an inward quest which, as a facet of the regenerative process, was to be completed only in heaven. In Taylor's meditations we discover, therefore, an individual and unique will creating pious poetry in imitation of, and hopefully in response to, Christ's love or grace as administered through his priestly and prophetic roles. Through the venting of this introspective search and the suspension of any conclusive judgment regarding his spiritual fate, Taylor derived from his love for Christ as much of a sense of regenerate self-identity as a Puritan could properly arrive at in this world.

i

The question of Taylor's mysticism is important. For Norman Grabo, the chief exponent of the mystical reading of Taylor's work, not only is the poet's "theory of poetry . . . derived from his mysticism," but "the mystical process is the subject" of his verse.[1] One of the difficulties of such a position lies in the word *mysticism;* owing to its reference to a wide range of beliefs and practices, the term is not easily defined. However, usually two types of mystical thought are identified: the one, according to which God is utterly outside and transcendent to the

1. *Edward Taylor*, pp. 43, 87. In spite of these comments, Grabo notes Taylor's refusal to identify with any consummation of a mystical union with Christ (pp. 82–83). Elsewhere Grabo argues that in the *Preparatory Meditations* "visions (imagined and actual) and sexual images abound, evidencing that Taylor reeled and staggered" ("The Veiled Vision: The Role of Aesthetics in Early American Intellectual History," *William and Mary Quarterly*, 19, October 1962, 505). Michael Colacurcio, on the other hand, remarks, "Taylor the pastoral rhetorician convinces me in a way that Taylor the would-be mystic does not" (*"Gods Determinations Touching Half-Way Membership:* Occasion and Audience in Edward Taylor," p. 313). The mystical aspect of Puritan thought is discussed at length by James F. Maclear, " 'The Heart of New England Rent': The Mystical Element in Early Puritan History," *Mississippi Valley Historical Review*, 41 (March 1956), 621–52.

universe man inhabits; the other, according to which God is immanent and dwells within creation, indeed within the very soul of man.

To be sure, certain particulars of both notions were incorporated in Puritan thought. Puritan divines construed God as a perfect and omnipotent Being, separate and distinct from his creation. Yet, they also saw the hand of divine Providence operating everywhere in their world, even in their personal lives. In fact, as we have seen, though they avoided heresy, they nevertheless believed that nature bears some intimate relation to its Creator. It was this latter conception which Perry Miller ascertained when he wrote: "there was in Puritanism a piety, a religious passion, the sense of an inward communication and of the divine symbolism of nature"; "at the core of the theology there was an indestructible element which was mystical, and a feeling for the universe which was almost pantheistic."[2]

Miller was careful to temper his comment concerning New England Puritan mysticism. There existed an *element* of it in their thought. This qualification, it seems to me, is likewise applicable to Taylor's verse, in which various particulars of mysticism occur. Besides his belief in God as perfect Being, as the only reality informing the universe, Taylor's effort to look within to discover truth and love as well as his tendency to reflect the Salesian spirit (emphasizing love and mental union)[3] in his meditations supports a mystical interpretation of his poems. It is also true that one can comb his verse and single out passages which can be made to conform with the traditional stages of mystical ascent: awakening, purification or purgation, illumination or rapture, the dark night of the soul, and spiritual marriage or union with God. Similarly, Taylor's fondness for metaphor and the circularity of so many of his images, if considered aside from his poetic decorum, buttress the mystical reading of his verse; for one of the implications of these two devices is that some underlying unity permeates all things.[4]

2. *Errand into the Wilderness*, p. 192.
3. Martz, *The Poetry of Meditation*, pp. 145–47.
4. Rosemond Tuve writes: "A mystical poem sees all sensible phenomena as meta-

Nevertheless, contrary evidence argues against a mystical interpretation of the *Preparatory Meditations*. For one thing, the purpose of meditation is not necessarily the preparation for a mystical experience. As Louis Martz has told us, meditation "is not, properly speaking, a mystical activity, but a part of the duties of everyone in daily life."[5] In other words, meditation, the practice designed to move the will or heart to God, is an outgrowth of as well as an inducement to the exercise of *practical* piety as the basis for the conduct of one's life in the temporal world.

The temporal world, as we saw in the first chapter, was not for Taylor an inherently demonic realm. He discerned there a progressive hierarchy of degrees of perfection and an innate goodness, founded on and pervaded by divine love, which denied the notion that a gap separates nature from heaven. As an heir of Augustinian thought he perceived not only that grace works through natural means but also that the order of nature participates in the order of grace; time is a part of eternity. Moreover, though it reflects the Son's image, the universe is no mere shadow; it is real insofar as it is imbued with God's Being or love, serves as the vehicle for the Incarnation, and is divinely ordained for man's use.

Thus Taylor did not advocate the abandonment of earthly things. All objects, rightly seen and properly used, point back to God, the source of their origin and their daily containment in being. This point of view is opposed to that of the mystic, whose aim remains "wholly transcendental and spiritual" and whose vision "is in no way concerned with adding to, explaining, rearranging, or improving anything in the visible universe."[6] Although Taylor certainly remonstrated against any disproportionate concern with or any misuse of the world and although he lamented the effects of man's Fall on nature, his

---

phor" (*Elizabethan and Metaphysical Imagery*, p. 219).

5. *The Poetry of Meditation*, p. 16.

6. Evelyn Underhill, *Mysticism*, p. 96. Augustine taught that "the more you love existence, the more you will desire eternal life. . . . The man who loves existence approves temporal things insofar as they exist" (*On Free Choice of the Will*, 3.7.72–73).

poetry evidences a conspicuous absence of the *contemptus mundi* motif usually associated with the thought of the mystic.

This conception of nature includes the human body. As we saw in the second chapter, Taylor not only discerned no gap between heaven and earth, but he also rejected the Platonic notion of a separation between the soul and its bodily instrument. To be sure, he often deplored the postlapsarian state of the fallen body, particularly the readiness of the sin-ridden will to play lackey to the flesh and thereby subvert the proper hierarchical relationship between them. He indeed knew that "the ill humors in the body will abide till this earthly tabernacle be dissolved," that as long as these ill humors persist as a result of the residence of sin in our wills, "we shall find these vermin crawling in our souls ofttimes, as worms in our bowels infesting our thoughts and sometimes crawling out in our discourse, and flyblowing our works, both civil and sacred concerns" (TCLS, p. 152). Yet Taylor is clear even in this metaphoric passage: it is its ill humors, its *fallen state*, not the body itself which is to be disparaged. The body always retains its original radical goodness, continues to share in the divine love pervading all creation; sin resides in the rational soul, which regulates the body and is superior to it. In fact, the desires and senses of the body are basically excellent; for initially they contributed to the expression of man's love for God and presently they are unruly only because of their misguidance by an unregenerate soul.

With this perspective it would have been unreasonable for Taylor to have advocated a mystical transcendence of the body. Choking off, repressing, or even seeking detachment from the senses and affections of the body were alien to his thought.[7] It would have been utterly inconsistent for the poet who devoted his entire adult life to singing the glory of the Incarnation—the event which, among other things, reasserted creation and elevat-

---

7. For the mystic's view of the flesh, see Underhill, *Mysticism*, pp. 205, 255, 264–65. Ludwig, who also reads Taylor as a mystic, writes: "The goal of mysticism has always been to transcend the cage of the flesh so that the soul will be free to return to the transcendent world from which it came" (*Graven Images*, pp. 48–49). But cf. Taylor's poem 1.8, 7–8.

ed the dignity of the flesh—to espouse mystical escape from the body. That would seem contrary to the observance of *imitatio Christi*, the practice Taylor explicitly emphasizes throughout his sermons and poems.

Likewise, though Taylor's central theme of his quest for love may seem at times to verge on the mystical, he always recognized that the pure love he was celebrating is unattainable on earth, that it is achieved only when the regenerative process is completed.[8] Thus Taylor's introspective search for this love never encouraged his withdrawal from the world or his escape to a "paradise within." Although his meditations were inward dramas, they actually reveal a self which remained fixed in a temporal context. I do not mean that these poems reflect a specific time and place—there are no explicit references to Westfield—but that they are permeated by man's world, his concerns, his tools, and the like. It is interesting to recall, in this regard, that Taylor assigned an exact date to most of the poems in the *Preparatory Meditations*.

The point to be drawn from these comments is that this context—it might well be termed a *historical* context—undercuts any sense of the traditional loss of the mystical poet's self. In the mystical experience "the self . . . surrenders itself, its individuality, and its will, completely" as "consciousness of I-hood and consciousness of the world disappear."[9] The will becomes totally passive, entirely overcome by the divine will.

This, however, is not the sort of surrender Taylor meant in regard to the will's regenerate relation to God's will. By the idea of the attunement of a saint's will to that of God Taylor did not imply that conversion negates or expunges the volitional faculty. On the contrary, in conjunction with its passive disposition to grace, the will is always to be actively expressed. The saint is no less an entity because he has been elected by God than was

8. Edwards defines pure love as a "union of the heart with others; a kind of enlargement of the mind, whereby it so extends itself as to take others into a man's self; and therefore it implies a disposition to feel, to desire, and to act as though others were one with ourselves" (*The Nature of True Virtue*, ed. William K. Frankena, p. 61).

9. Underhill, *Mysticism*, pp. 206, 371, 374.

Christ's manhood less than human because it was joined to Godhead. When attuned by grace, the will is *renewed;* that, in fact, is the whole point. Renewal through divine love constitutes the saint's true self or identity. Without this grace the will, the pivotal faculty of the whole man or self, remains powerless, empty. That is to say, without the renewal of God's image and love in the soul, a man's self is virtually nonexistent; without grace it fails to share in a meaningful way in the radical Being or love pervading creation. But when Christ marries or attunes a will, he elevates it, just as his incarnation added dignity to the flesh. Through the artistry of grace he engenders love of God, thereby giving the saint's self a basis for meaning, for identity.

This focus on the will and the theme of love, when read in the light of Taylor's poetic decorum, counters any idea of a loss of self in mystical silence. In order to respond to the Word, the Poet of poets, Taylor imitated the Logos and asserted his will or self verbally. Not silence but words, the primary mode of this assertion of the will, express and define the poet's self. Taylor suspended this expression of his self in the verbal bridge he built to God through the Word. There, he hoped, it arched within the mediating crosscurrents of mutual love. There too lay the key to his spiritual state, his temporal judgment of which likewise hung suspended. Poem after poem concludes in future tense, in subjunctive mode, in petition rather than in resolution, for Taylor eschewed a simple or easy deciphering of the complex matter of his spiritual condition. Because he believed that "we are in the way of ordinary dispensations, and therefore are not to expect extraordinary communications" (TCLS, p. 157), he never crossed the bridge of his verbal piety into the blinding light and numbing silence of mystical assurance and union.

ii

In the light of this emphasis on the existence of his self in an experiential context, a few words should be said on Taylor's temporal role as minister and poet. Though these two vocations include all three modes of the heart's expression, they primarily relate to the use of words, which as we have seen, was especially relevant to Taylor's view of the will. As the expression of a minister, Taylor's public or spoken words became works and deeds. They constituted the tools of logic, the instruments of reason to be applied to the understandings of his parishioners. Were these words successful agents in planting the seed of faith in a single heart, then they would have performed a double function: they would have not only served as a channel or conduit of grace from God but they would have also, as it were, linked the soul to Christ. This is to say that Taylor's principle of decorum did not apply solely to his poetry; it also informed his interpretation of his ministerial duties.[10]

As the expression of a poet, Taylor's private or written words of interior meditation dealt with the will more than with the understanding.[11] Thomas Hooker, employing an image for words similar to that used by Taylor, explained the relation between the public sermon and the private meditation when he wrote that the language of "Application is like the Conduit or channel that brings the stream of the Truth upon the soul; but Meditation stops it as it were, and makes it soak into the heart."[12] The preacher's sermon should like grace itself stimulate a private verbal response within. From this vantage point we might speculate that Taylor similarly perceived a sequential

10. Reinforcing certain of Perry Miller's conclusions, Keith L. Sprunger comments that in Puritan thought "There was no art without its eupraxia, and no discipline which was merely contemplative" ("Technometria: A Prologue to Puritan Theology," *Journal of the History of Ideas*, 29, January-March 1968, 118).

11. On the question of Taylor's attitude toward the publication of his verse, see Grabo, *Edward Taylor*, p. 174; Emma Shepherd, "Edward Taylor's Injunction Against Publication," *American Literature*, 33 (January 1962), 512–13; Donald E. Stanford, *Edward Taylor*, University of Minnesota Pamphlets on American Writers, no. 52, p. 6; Clark Griffith, "Edward Taylor and the Momentum of Metaphor," *ELH*, 33 (December 1966), 460. See especially Francis Murphy, "Edward Taylor's Attitude toward Publication: A Question Concerning Authority," *American Literature*, 34 (November 1962), 393–94; Charles W. Mignon, "Some Notes on the History of the Edward Taylor Manuscripts," *Yale University Library Gazette*, 39 (April 1965), 168–73; and Keller, "The Example of Edward Taylor," pp. 5-26. Colacurcio makes some interesting comments regarding the question of audience in *Gods Determinations* ("*Gods Determinations Touching Half-Way Membership*: Occasion and Audience in Edward Taylor," p. 300).

12. *The Application of Redemption*, p. 214; see also Haller, *The Rise of Puritanism*, p. 115.

relation between his verse and his sermons. We might further judge that, owing to the superiority of meditation over the sermon, Taylor considered verse to be more suitable than discursive prose to express his will.[13]

Norman Grabo has postulated the theory that Taylor drafted the sacrament-day sermon first and then wrote the poem which described the poet's emotional response to the doctrine of the sermon.[14] Such poetic expression may in fact have provided a means of preparation for the actual delivery of the sermon. Although this is an uncertain conclusion, this sequence is consistent with Augustine's teaching and with the Puritan tradition that a minister should privately prepare himself before giving his sermon.[15] For Taylor this threefold sequence may have embodied the will's three modes of response. In composing the sermon

13. Edwards wrote: "the duty of singing praises to God, seems to be appointed wholly to excite and express religious affections. No other reason can be assigned, why we should express ourselves to God in verse, rather than in prose" (*Religious Affections*, p. 115). See also Tuve, *Elizabethan and Metaphysical Imagery*, p. 398.

14. "Introduction," c, pp. xxxiv–xxxv and Grabo's "Catholic Tradition, Puritan Literature, and Edward Taylor," *Papers of the Michigan Academy of Science, Arts, and Letters*, 45 (1960), 401–2. Donald E. Stanford (review of *Edward Taylor's Christographia, American Literature*, 35, May 1963, 242–3), E. F. Carlisle ("The Puritan Structure of Edward Taylor's Poetry," 48–49), and Donald A. Junkins ("Edward Taylor's Creative Process," *Early American Literature*, 4, Winter 1970, 67–78) concur with Grabo. However, concerning Grabo's conclusion that "the poems are based not on the text that precedes them but on the doctrine drawn from that text" (c, p. xxxiv), Robert M. Benton disagrees: "the texts form the basis of the sermons and, in a parallel but independent manner, the basis of the poems" ("Edward Taylor's Use of His Text," *American Literature*, 39, March 1967, 32). Also it should be noted that Thomas M. Davis has argued that not only this sequence but the very relation of these poems to the sacrament-day sermon is untenable ("Edward Taylor's 'Occasional Meditations,' " pp. 17–29). Davis' points deserve attention but remain inconclusive. The erratic dating of the *Preparatory Meditations* may be deceptive. We know, for instance, that some of Taylor's poems have been lost. It is also likely that Taylor may have deleted and destroyed any number of them, for it is clear that he reread and revised them from time to time. All we know for certain is Taylor's own title: *Preparatory Meditations before my Approach to the Lords Supper. Chiefly upon the Doctrin preached upon the Day of administration.*

15. The Christian orator will succeed "more through the piety of his prayers than through the skill of his oratory, so that, praying for himself and for those whom he is to address, he is a petitioner before he is a speaker" (Augustine, *On Christian Doctrine*, 4.15.32). See also Hooker, *The Application of Redemption*, p. 204.

he would have concentrated on his reason (thought), in writing the poem he would have focused on his will (word), and in delivering the sermon he would have exerted his whole being in the service of God (deed). Since thought, word, and deed are equivalent modes of the language of the heart, this sequence may have given Taylor the conviction that by using words in the combined exercise of his ministerial and poetic duties he was complying with his complete vocation.

Even if we are correct in our assumption, it is doubtful that Taylor always adhered to such a procedure. Various exigencies would have time and again interfered, and the extant poems will not permit any easy generalization. Yet, it is likely, on the other hand, that whenever he did write such a poem, the place of the meditation was central to the sequence. Poem after poem opens with a quest for words and ends with an active effort on the part of the poet to submit his will to God's loving attunement. If the art of grace were to empower his heart, then the words of his sermon would become the vehicles of that art of love to others: "My kirnell ripe shall rattle out thy praise / And Orient blush on my actions blaze" (2.47, 35–36). Taylor means that with the Word's art he will sing, albeit imperfectly (rattle), God's praise in his poems. But since in order to do so his will must be in tune with the divine will and since words, conceived in that will, are the instruments of grace, the art of the Logos will be reflected not only in his poetry but also in his ministerial action of delivering the sermon.

Taylor, therefore, may have drawn an analogy between the operation of the will and his meditations. Perhaps his meditations were meant to reflect the will's union of the soul and body, of reason and affections, and also to mediate in some sense between the composition (thought) and the delivery (deed) of the sermon. To be sure, these poems do record Taylor's desire to imitate the Word's mediatory role, and this effort doubtless informed his ministerial actions (works are words) as well. Indeed, he held that since Christ is in regard to words and deeds "the most perfect Coppy to write after," everyone should "Strive to

159

hold forth the Glory of the Person of Christ in [his] Christian life, and Conversation" (C, pp. 167, 104).

We might conclude, furthermore, that Taylor sought to imitate Christ's offices as priest and prophet. As a priest—free from any Anglican or Roman Catholic context, of course—as the leader of worship, Taylor mediated Godward for his parishioners. Similar to Christ in His "Priestly office," Taylor's duty was to "transact the Concerns of men with God"; for in a restricted sense he too was "ordain'd for men in those things which are to be acted with God" (C, p. 338; cf. Rev. 1: 6). As a prophet, especially as defined by Saint Paul (1 Cor. 14), Taylor was called to mediate manward as an ambassador of Christ, to entreat and beseech men "in Christs Stead to be reconciled to God" (C, p. 338).[16] Like the biblical prophets, it was less his task to forecast the future or even to philosophize than to preach, to utilize himself as a poet of contemplation and as a ministerial man of action called to be a historical agent of God. The fulfillment of both callings requires the presence of the Holy Spirit in the will.

Although the priestly intercession from man to God was a part of his ministerial duty, it was preceded in sequence and in importance by the prophetic office of *ministerium verbi divini*. For the soul had first to be the passive recipient of grace before it was empowered to respond actively; and the minister's words served as the channels of this grace, thereby, so to speak, bridging heaven and earth. In this sense Taylor's private meditations prepared him to execute his public, prophetic duty. Hence these poems at times allude to the election of the prophet Isaiah (Isa. 4: 7 –9). Images of the burning coal which purifies the heart and lips frequently appear in the *Preparatory Meditations*, for were he touched by the coal of converting grace, Taylor would be enabled to act as prophet. Thus he implored, "In mee / A beame of thy Prophet-icke Sun imploy" (2.54, 44–45); "if thy Altars Coale Enfire my heart, / With this Blesst Life my Soule will be thy Sparke" (2.82, 11–12; see also 2.86, 7–9; 2.92, 3–4):

16. These two offices are also defined in the Westfield "Church Record," pp. 39–40. In *Some Thoughts Concerning the Present Revival of Religion in New-England* Edwards argues that the minister represents Christ's person in these two roles.

> Lord, let a Seraphim a live Coale take
> Off of thine Altar, with it touch my lips.
> And purge away my Sins for mercys sake.
>
> (2.49, 26–28)

With the burning coal of grace his heart would be enkindled, and with his will thus attuned, he would be able to express prophetically the divine Will; by opening the word of God to others he would be imitating Christ's mediatory office. Then the pious expression of his heart's love in poems and sermons would better enable him to tend Christ's "Sacred selfe with Sacred art" (2.36, 40). He would be imitating Christ not by the experience of flights of mystical ecstasy but through the assertion of his renewed and dedicated self in thought, word, and deed in the world of daily life.

iii

What emerges from the *Preparatory Meditations* is a portrait of Taylor's incessant endeavor to assert his self and to appraise that self's relation to the "Sacred selfe." In one way or another these are the concerns reiterated throughout American literature. American writing again and again reflects an unqualified moral intensity, a quest for meaning in relation to something greater than man (whether it be God or some ideal), a symbolical reading of the surfaces of life, a sense of the participation of time in the timeless, and a proclivity to construe art as symbolic scriptures of the self. It is principally in regard to this last pattern that Taylor belongs to the American tradition. In the introspective probing of his meditations—however entrenched they may be in theology—he reflects the American fascination with identity, with exploring the inner life of the self.

The carefully dated poems of the *Preparatory Meditations* stem from what Taylor called "an inward Search" or "heart examination," and they can rightly be said to present an autobiography of Taylor's self. If he were one of Christ's elect, the very words of these poems would become the narrative of his conversion, a true spiritual relation of the turning of his heart and its love; for

161

confession of this sort can signify the inner depths of God's work on the soul. True confession is motivated not by an assenting reason but by a will which has fully consented and is now responding to divine love. Taylor believed, in accord with Renaissance thought, that since words reveal the state of one's mind or soul, an image of his true identity must be mirrored in his writings. This relation between language and the self informs the following lines: "I am Tonguetide stupid, sensless stand, / And Drier drain'd than is my pen I hand"; with Christ's all-filling art of grace, "I then shall sweetly tune thy Praise, When hee / In whom all Fulness dwells, doth dwell in mee" (1.27, 11–12, 47–48). The pen represents an extension, a tool of the poet's will. The words it writes by his hand simultaneously discover and express his self. Indeed, the necessity of defining his self through words pervades Taylor's verse and provides an answer as to why the *Preparatory Meditations* steadily focuses on the will and treats the theme of love.

To recapitulate briefly: Taylor adhered to the view that grace or divine love enters the soul through reason and finally resides in the will, which must actively consent to submit passively to God's will. The result of this reception of grace is the partial restoration of the divine image lost by Adam's Fall. Grace puts the "Heart in kilter" (2.6, 4); it attunes the will to the divine will. Since the will is the verbalizing power, its expression in thought, word, and deed—which for Taylor were equivalent modes of the language of the heart—reflects its spiritual condition. Words, which subsume thoughts and deeds, are containers of will. They reveal the presence or absence of God's imprint upon the soul. Thus, if Taylor were granted grace, his work, the employment of words as poet and minister, would inevitably reflect Christ's art: "My heart, thy harp, make, and thy Grace my string. / Thy Glory then shall be my Song I'l sing" (2.102, 41–42); "I'le sacrifice to thee my Heart in praise, / When thy Rich Grace shall be my hearty Phrase" (2.6, 53–54).

Christ's art of love, in other words, generates a response. Just as divine art conveys love to the recipient heart, so also the saint reciprocates in pious art stimulated by its love, the fundamental affection of a will renewed by grace. The divine love engendering Christ's marriage of the soul begets love in turn; for concerning all marriages "God strictly commands *mutual love* in this Relation."[17] The artistic words of the poet-saint will mirror the art of the Word; in fact, they will progressively reflect a "growing Grace"—more and more grace; an increasing degree of verbal gracefulness—back to God (2.13, 48): "My Love to thee advance till it Commence / In all Degrees of Love, a Graduate high" (2.40, 39–40). With this progressive experience of divine love— an experience in harmony with the law of nature, according to which everything moves along a heirarchy of degrees—the saint is, in terms of Taylor's imagery, slowly fashioned into a gem which derives its radiance from the sun (Son) and mirrors this brillance and sparkle back to its source. True love and the holy art it stimulates belong only to the regenerate. Taylor thus looked to his gemlike words ("Prologue," 1. 30) for an image or reflection of this art of grace.

For Taylor, therefore, verbal piety was, on the one hand, the means of responding to his vocation to use words publicly in the craft of his sermons. It comprised, on the other hand, a private and inward exploration of the moral state of his soul. In both capacities—that is, as the mean between action and contemplation—the assertion of the self in words was to imitate the mediatory role of the Logos. In order to communicate to God his personal concerns, which *Gods Determinations* makes clear are those of every man, Taylor devised a poetic decorum according to which style and metaphor reflect the Word's union of Godhead and manhood. He expressed, appropriately enough, the relation of this pious artistry to the Word in literary terms: by means of divine love, the art of grace, Christ must first "in golden Letters write" upon the soul a "Superscription in an Holy style" (1.6, 15–16); the poet will then strive to "spell out therein" and to "read, and read" this message (2.8, 38, 41). Thus inspired, the poet's artistry will "display" divine "Glory through't" ("Prologue," ll. 21–22) until, in heaven, he fully tends the "Lord in all admiring Style."

17. Benjamin Wadsworth, *The Well-Ordered Family*, p. 42.

Although he stressed the dependence of his will upon grace for the power to express itself in true pious art, Taylor never obscured the importance of the active efforts of his poetic self, either in preparing for or responding to grace. Grace does not rape the will; it weds the heart in such a way that the saint never loses his identity. Consequently, he should not seek to escape his earthbound self through mystical transcendence.[18] For this self must assert its love verbally, not in spite of but *because* of its conversion and attunement to God's will. With his will thus in tune, the saint's verbal piety unveils his inner self just as the Word represents the divine Self. Therefore, while it is true that for Taylor "meaning is what matters, and this world gets its meaning wholly from outside,"[19] one should not fail to stress as well the internal medium of the poet's will in regard to the realization or actualization of this meaning.

This self, however, remains suspended between presumption and despair, for the regenerative process is completed only in heaven. The saint must consequently forswear a sense of certitude and assurance: "Doubtings and faith may stande and will stand together."[20] In the temporal world God's ways are continuous and progressive.[21] Christ is "forever beginning in . . . [the] soul" as that soul experiences "all Degrees of Love." Though divine fullness certainly "runs to and fro" in a manner quite different from the ebb and flow of the tides (2.51, 31–34), man's response to Christ's love—grace, as we have seen, is depicted as a fluid, as *Aqua Vitae*, throughout Taylor's verse—does fluctuate. Because it is less perfect than Christ's love, the saint's love appropriately reflects the ocean's tidal movements. On earth no one

18. Kathleen Blake notes that "Taylor's 'wedden feast,' the highest instance of man's communion with God, is an espousal, not a consummation. Man and God . . . do not transfuse, or transubstantiate: the higher reality does not consume or obliterate the lower" ("Edward Taylor's Protestant Poetic," pp. 18–19).

19. Waggoner, "Edward Taylor," p. 20.

20. "Theological Notes," p. 27[v].

21. Speaking of Augustine's view of this concept, Roger Hazelton remarks: "Relatedness to God is not a position but a movement, not a point but a process. No static confrontation but a dynamic interaction of the soul and God is its substance, realized with a moving, growing experience" ("The Devotional Life," in *A Companion to the Study of St. Augustine*, p. 401).

evidences a constant response (see Taylor's "The Ebb and Flow"), and the affections of the will seem very much like the tides.[22]

But just as the earthly tides represent a uniform or fixed rhythm, the saint's alternation between hope and despair signifies the underlying constancy of God's scheme. It reflects the continuation of the process initiated at the time of creation, when divine love flowed from God's hand in a fluid genesis. So the apparent inconsistency of the saint's heart may in reality be "blessed motions" in disguise (GD, p. 432). In *Gods Determinations* even Satan, unaware that he is a mere pen in the hand of Providence, seizes upon this very image, thereby inadvertently explaining God's ways to the very saints he is trying to torment:

> What's thy Repentance? Can'st thou come and show
> By those salt Rivers which do Ebb, and Flow
> By th'motion of that Ocean Vast within,
> Of pickled sorrow rising for thy Sin?   (p. 412)

The saint, of course, cannot answer this question. He must always contend with doubt and a distraught conscience in the temporal world. Only God knows for certain who is saved.

But the saint is not left without hope; this same inconclusiveness or incompleteness is, in Taylor's view, a part of the divine plan. The very *drama* of conversion in fact lies in this process. In order to avoid violating a man's self or will, God makes the drama progressive. As we noted in the third chapter, in spite of Christ's "Sea of Electing Grace, and Love," the saint continues to be tossed amid the "Worlds wild waves." The elect still experience in their daily lives a sense of drifting between the lures of Satan's perverse, disdainful logic and the assurances conveyed by Christ's promises. This rhythmic restlessness of the anguished conscience carries men to God, with whom true peace of mind

22. Cotton used the same image: "Though you might thinke the sands would soone be fretted through by the boysterous waves, yet God by his word hath made the sand a perpetuall Bulwarke against the sea, that it cannot prevaile against it; but the heart of man is more unruly then the great sea, and more illimitable then the sea" (*The Way of Life*, p. 204).

165

resides; for, as we have previously noted, it is the intent of Providence to reserve "something that is the most concerning, as the *ultima lima* of glory last attained unto, as an allurement." It is this attraction, this drama of the self wrestling for true identity in Christ, which is at the vital core of Taylor's poems.

Thus, in spite of the fact that he had experienced a spiritual awakening at an early age, that he felt called as a minister of Christ, and that he believed some degree of assurance of one's election could eventually be attained, Taylor realized that decisive insight into "that Ocean Vast within" was known with certitude only by God. Of the three principal stages of the "instituted order that God attends in converting souls from sin to Himself" (TCLS, p. 99), he had experienced a partial "enlightening" of his reason and a "convicting" of his conscience. But he continually inquired as to the "turning" of his heart. Even in his public "Spiritual Relation" delivered on August 27, 1679, Taylor admitted, concerning the turning of his heart, that he could only discover "Something of this nature," that the affection of love was "more Sensible at one time than at another."[23] Thus his meditative explorations of the heart finally left the issue of his spiritual condition unresolved, especially since a sense of confidence might testify to damning presumption. The judgment of the moral state of his soul had to be held in abeyance. So he suspended his expectations across his verbal bridge to God, hoping that they were bathed in the crosscurrents of the "mutuall Intrest" of shared love flowing to and fro through "that Golden Linck" of Christ.

In fact, when the reader realizes that Taylor wrote the *Preparatory Meditations* over a span of forty-three years (1682–1725), he is struck by their static quality. In spite of some thematic variety, there is, generally speaking, no development, no divergence, no progress in the thought or artistry of his verse.[24] Tedious as it

23. Stanford, "Edward Taylor's 'Spiritual Relation,'" pp. 469, 474.
24. Charles W. Mignon discusses "the unchanging character of the speaker's attitude" in the *Preparatory Meditations* in relation to Taylor's wavering between doubt and certitude in "A Principle of Order in Edward Taylor's *Preparatory Meditations*," *Early American Literature*, 4 (Winter 1970), 110–16. However, this observation has been incon-

often becomes, this unchanging character of the entire corpus of the *Preparatory Meditations* derived from the poet's basic irresolution. It grew out of his refusal to decide whether or not the ebb and flow of his love, as evidenced in the rhythm of his verbal piety, mirrored the influence of the regenerating waters, the *Aqua Vitae*, of the Word's art. He patiently awaited, albeit not without anxiety, the unfolding of God's plan. After death, each man's

> Wildred state will wane away, and hence
> These Crooked Passages will soon appeare
> The Curious needlework of Providence,
> Embrodered with golden Spangles Cleare.
> Judge not this Web while in the Loom, but stay
> From judging it untill the judgment day.
>
> For while its foiled up the best Can see
> But little of it, and that little too
> Shews weather beaten but when it shall bee
> Hung open all at once, Oh beautious shew!
> Though threds run in, and out, Cross snarld and twinde
> The Web will even be enwrought you'l finde.

(GD, pp. 449–50)

This anchoring of his will in God's mysterious but certain design and the consequent suspension of his individual and assertive self across a bridge of verbal piety founded on the mediation of the Logos or Christ, in whom all true identity lies, are what the *Preparatory Meditations* is finally about.

In his quest for saving identity amidst Puritan theological thought, psychological notions, and literary traditions, Taylor created the best poetry to emerge from seventeenth-century New England culture. It is generally true that we tend to recall or linger over certain striking, beautiful, even remarkable lines or stanzas rather than the somewhat sprawling entirety of the individual poems. Nevertheless, considered as a whole, the *Preparatory*

---

clusively questioned by Gene Russell, "Dialectal and Phonetic Features of Edward Taylor's Rhymes: A Brief Study Based upon a Computer Concordance of His Poems," *American Literature*, 43 (May 1971), 165–80.

Meditations still impresses us. We are moved less by any display of poetic pyrotechnics than by Taylor's unequivocal commitment to his inward quest for love, conversion, identity—for Being, eternal life. The intensity of his search redeems the times we are put off by some disproportion, starkness, impropriety or mismanagement; more often than not the reader is provoked to some deeper level of consent. We too are charmed by "the Lisping Child." We come to value the legacy of Edward Taylor's poetry for numerous reasons, not the least of which is its heartfelt, personal narrative of an ingrained faith and an unwavering devotion rarely possible for us today.

Works Cited

Alexis, Gerhard T. "Jonathan Edwards and the Theocratic Ideal." *Church History*, 35 (September 1966), 328–43.

Augustine. *The Advantage of Believing*. Translated by Luanna Meagher. In *The Fathers of the Church*. Vol. 2, pp. 381–442. New York: CIMA, 1947.

————. *The City of God*. Translated by Marcus Dods. 2 vols. Edinburgh, Scot.: T & T Clark, 1872.

————. *Confessions*. Translated by R. S. Pine-Coffin. London: Penguin, 1961.

————. *Divine Providence and the Problem of Evil*. Translated by Robert P. Russell. In *The Fathers of the Church*. Vol. 1, pp. 227–332. New York: CIMA, 1948.

————. *The Greatness of the Soul*. Translated by Joseph M. Colleran. In *Ancient Christian Writers*. Vol. 9, pp. 1–112. Westminster, Md.: Newman Press, 1950.

————. *Omnium operum*. Paris, 1531–1532.

————. *On Free Choice of the Will*. Translated by Anna S. Benjamin and L. H. Hackstaff. New York: Bobbs-Merrill, 1964.

————. *On Christian Doctrine*. Translated by D. W. Robertson. New York: Liberal Arts Press, 1958.

————. *The Teacher*. Translated by Joseph M. Colleran. In *Ancient Christian Writers*. Vol. 9, pp. 113–86. Westminster, Md.: Newman Press, 1950.

Works Cited

―――. *The Trinity*. Translated by Stephen McKenna. In *The Fathers of the Church*. Vol. 45. Washington, D.C.: Catholic University of America, 1963.

Baker, Herschel. *The Wars of Truth: Studies in the Decay of Christian Humanism in the Earlier Seventeenth Century*. Cambridge: Harvard University Press, 1952.

Ball, Kenneth R. "Rhetoric in Edward Taylor's *Preparatory Meditations*." *Early American Literature*, 4 (Winter 1970), 79–88.

Ballinger, Martha. "The Metaphysical Echo." *English Studies in Africa*, 8 (March 1965), 71–80.

Barker, Arthur E. "Structural and Doctrinal Pattern in Milton's Later Poems." In *Essays in English Literature from the Renaissance to the Victorian Age*. Edited by Miller MacLure and F. W. Watt, pp. 169–194. Toronto: University of Toronto Press, 1964.

Battenhouse, Roy W. "The Doctrine of Man in Calvin and in Renaissance Platonism." *Journal of the History of Ideas*, 9 (October 1948), 447–71.

―――, ed. *A Companion to the Study of St. Augustine*. New York: Oxford University Press, 1955.

Baxter, Richard. *The Saints Everlasting Rest*. London: Religious Tract Society, 1841.

Benton, Robert M. "Edward Taylor's Use of His Text." *American Literature*, 39 (March 1967), 31–41.

Black, Mindele. "Edward Taylor: Heavens Sugar Cake." *New England Quarterly*, 29 (June 1956), 159–81.

Blake, Howard. "Seventeenth-Century Yankee." *Poetry*, 56 (June 1940), 165–69.

Blake, Kathleen. "Edward Taylor's Protestant Poetic: Nontransubstantiating Metaphor." *American Literature*, 43 (March 1971), 1–24.

Blau, Herbert. "Heaven's Sugar Cake: Theology and Imagery in the Poetry of Edward Taylor." *New England Quarterly*, 26 (September 1953), 337–60.

Boll, Robert, and Thomas M. Davis. "Saint Augustine and Edward Taylor's Meditation 138 (2)." *English Language Notes*, 8 (March 1971), 183–85.

Brown, Wallace C. "Edward Taylor: An American 'Metaphysical.'" *American Literature*, 16 (November 1944), 186–97.

Bushman, Richard L. *From Puritan to Yankee: Character and the Social Order in Connecticut, 1690–1765*. Cambridge: Harvard University Press, 1967.

Callow, James T. "Edward Taylor Obeys Saint Paul." *Early American Literature*, 4 (Winter 1970), 89–96.

Calvin, John. *Institutes of the Christian Religion*. Translated by Ford L. Battles. 2 vols. London: SCM Press, 1961.

Carlisle, E. F. "The Puritan Structure of Edward Taylor's Poetry." *American Quarterly*, 20 (Summer 1968), 147–63.

Cochrane, Charles N. *Christianity and Classical Culture: A Study of Thought and Action from Augustus to Augustine*. Oxford: Clarendon Press, 1940.

Colacurcio, Michael J. *"Gods Determinations Touching Half-Way Membership:* Occasion and Audience in Edward Taylor." *American Literature,* 39 (November 1967), 298–314.

Cotton, John. *The Covenant of Grace: Discovering the Great Work of a Sinners Reconciliation to God.* London, 1655.

————. *The Way of Life.* London, 1641.

Davidson, Edward H. *Jonathan Edwards: The Narrative of a Puritan Mind.* 1966. Reprint. Cambridge: Harvard University Press, 1968.

Davis, Thomas M. "Edward Taylor and the Traditions of Puritan Typology." *Early American Literature,* 4 (Winter 1970), 27–47.

————. "Edward Taylor's 'Occasional Meditations.' " *Early American Literature,* 5 (Winter 1971), 17–29.

Davis, Thomas M. and Virginia L. Davis. "Edward Taylor on the Day of Judgment." *American Literature,* 43 (January 1972), 525–47.

————. "Edward Taylor's Library: Another Note." *Early American Literature,* 6 (Winter 1972), 271–73.

dePauley, William C. *The Candle of the Lord: Studies in the Cambridge Platonists.* London: Society for Promoting Christian Knowledge, 1937.

Donne, John. *Sermons.* Edited by George Potter and Evelyn Simpson. 10 vols. Berkeley: University of California Press, 1953.

"Edward Taylor to Increase Mather." *Collections of the Massachusetts Historical Society,* 4th series, 8 (1868), 629–31.

Edwards, Jonathan. *Freedom of the Will.* Edited by Paul Ramsey. New Haven: Yale University Press, 1957.

————. *Jonathan Edwards: Representative Selections.* Edited by Clarence H. Faust and Thomas H. Johnson. Rev. ed. New York: Hill & Wang, 1962.

————. *"The Mind" of Jonathan Edwards.* Edited by Leon Howard. University of California Studies, No. 28. Berkeley, 1963.

————. *The Nature of True Virtue.* Edited by William K. Frankena. Ann Arbor: University of Michigan Press, 1960.

————. *Original Sin.* Edited by Clyde A. Holbrook. New Haven: Yale University Press, 1970.

————. *Some Thoughts Concerning the Present Revival of Religion in New-England.* In *The Great Awakening.* Edited by C. C. Goen, pp. 289–530. New Haven: Yale University Press, 1972.

————. *A Treatise Concerning Religious Affections.* Edited by John E. Smith. New Haven: Yale University Press, 1959.

————. *An Unpublished Essay of Edwards on the Trinity.* Edited by George P. Fisher. New York: Scribner's, 1903.

————. *The Works of President Edwards.* Edited by S. Austin. 1808. Reprint. New York: Leavitt & Allen, 1856.

Elwood, Douglas J. *The Philosophical Theology of Jonathan Edwards.* New York:

Works Cited

Columbia University Press, 1960.

Emerson, Everett H. "Calvin and Covenant Theology." *Church History*, 25 (June 1956), 136–44.

Fender, Stephen. "Edward Taylor and 'The Application of Redemption.' " *Modern Language Review*, 59 (July 1964), 331–34.

Fitch, James. *The First P[r]inciples of the Doctrine of Christ*. Boston, 1679.

Frederick, John T. "Literary Art in Thomas Hooker's *The Poor Doubting Christian*." *American Literature*, 40 (March 1968), 1–8.

Gay, Peter. *A Loss of Mastery: Puritan Historians in Colonial America*. Berkeley: University of California Press, 1966.

Goodman, William B. "Edward Taylor Writes His Love." *New England Quarterly*, 27 (December 1954), 510–15.

Grabo, Norman S. "'The Appeale Tried': Another Edward Taylor Manuscript." *American Literature*, 34 (November 1962), 394–400.

———. "Catholic Tradition, Puritan Literature, and Edward Taylor." *Papers of the Michigan Academy of Science, Arts, and Letters*, 45 (1960), 395–402.

———. *Edward Taylor*. New York: Twayne, 1961.

———. "Edward Taylor on the Lord's Supper." *Boston Public Library Quarterly*, 12 (January 1960), 22–36.

———. "Edward Taylor's Spiritual Huswifery." *PMLA*, 79 (December 1964), 554–60.

———. "The Poet to the Pope: Edward Taylor to Solomon Stoddard." *American Literature*, 32 (May 1960), 197–201.

———. "The Veiled Vision: The Role of Aesthetics in Early American Intellectual History." *William and Mary Quarterly*, 19 (October 1962), 493–510.

———, ed. *Edward Taylor's Christographia*. New Haven: Yale University Press, 1962. Originally "Edward Taylor's *Christographia* Sermons: Edited from the Manuscript with a Discussion of Their Relationship to His 'Sacramental Meditations.' " Ph.D. dissertation, University of California, 1958.

———, ed. *Edward Taylor's Treatise Concerning the Lord's Supper*. East Lansing: Michigan State University Press, 1965.

Griffith, Clark. "Edward Taylor and the Momentum of Metaphor." *ELH*, 33 (December 1966), 448–60.

Halbert, Cecelia L. "Tree of Life Imagery in the Poetry of Edward Taylor." *American Literature*, 38 (March 1966), 22–34.

Haller, William. *The Rise of Puritanism*. New York: Columbia University Press, 1938. Reprint. New York: Harper & Row, 1957.

Hooker, Thomas. *The Application of Redemption*. London, 1657.

Hoopes, Robert. *Right Reason in the English Renaissance*. Cambridge: Harvard University Press, 1962.

Jantz, Harold S. "The First Native-Born Group." *The First Century of New England Verse. Proceedings of the American Antiquarian Society*, 53 (20 October 1943), 295–301. Reprint. Worcester, Mass.: American Antiquarian Society, 1944, pp. 79–85.

Jeanes, Henry. *A Mixture of Scholasticall Divinity*. Oxford, 1656.

Johnson, Thomas H. "Edward Taylor: A Puritan 'Sacred Poet.' " *New England Quarterly*, 10 (June 1937), 290–322.

———. "Some Edward Taylor Gleanings." *New England Quarterly*, 16 (June 1943), 280–96.

———. "The Topical Verses of Edward Taylor." *Publications of the Colonial Society of Massachusetts*, 34 (February 1942), 513–54.

———, ed. *The Poetical Works of Edward Taylor*. New York: Rockland Editions, 1939. Reprint. Princeton, N.J.: Princeton University Press, 1943, 1966.

Junkins, Donald A. "Edward Taylor's Creative Process." *Early American Literature*, 4 (Winter 1970), 67–78.

———. "Edward Taylor's Revisions." *American Literature*, 37 (May 1965), 135–52.

———. " 'Should Stars Wooe Lobster Claws?': A Study of Edward Taylor's Poetic Practice and Theory." *Early American Literature*, 3 (Fall 1968), 88–117.

Kaufmann, U. Milo. *The Pilgrim's Progress and Traditions in Puritan Meditation*. New Haven: Yale University Press, 1966.

Keller, Karl. "The Example of Edward Taylor." *Early American Literature*, 4 (Winter 1970), 5–26.

Lockwood, John H. *A Sermon Commemorative of the Two-Hundredth Anniversary of the First Congregational Church of Westfield, Mass*. Westfield: Clark & Story, 1879.

———. *Westfield and Its Historic Influences: 1669–1919: The Life of an Early Town*. 1:106–72. Springfield, Mass.: Springfield Printing & Binding Co., 1922.

Lovejoy, Arthur O. *The Great Chain of Being*. Cambridge: Harvard University Press, 1936.

Ludwig, Allan I. *Graven Images: New England Stonecarving and Its Symbols, 1650–1815*. Middletown, Conn.: Wesleyan University Press, 1966.

Maclear, James F. " 'The Heart of New England Rent': The Mystical Element in Early Puritan History." *Mississippi Valley Historical Review*, 41 (March 1956), 621–52.

Madsen, William G. "The Idea of Nature in Milton's Poetry." *Three Studies in the Renaissance: Sidney, Jonson, Milton*, pp. 181–283. New Haven: Yale University Press, 1958.

Martz, Louis L. *The Poetry of Meditation: A Study of English Religious Literature of the Seventeenth Century*. 1954. Rev. ed. New Haven: Yale University Press, 1962.

Works Cited

————, ed. *The Meditative Poem: An Anthology of Seventeenth-Century Verse*, pp. 485–517. Garden City: Doubleday, 1963.

Mather, Cotton. *Right Thoughts in Sad Hours*. London, 1689.

Mather, Increase. *The Mystery of Christ*. Boston, 1686.

McAlindon, T. "Language, Style, and Meaning in *Troilus and Cressida*." *PMLA*, 84 (January 1969), 29–43.

Middlekauff, Robert. "Piety and Intellect in Puritanism." *William and Mary Quarterly*, 22 (July 1965), 457–70.

Mignon, Charles W. "Diction in Edward Taylor's 'Preparatory Meditations.'" *American Speech*, 41 (December 1966), 243–53.

————. "Edward Taylor's *Preparatory Meditations*: A Decorum of Imperfection." *PMLA*, 83 (October 1968), 1423–28.

————. "A Principle of Order in Edward Taylor's *Preparatory Meditations*." *Early American Literature*, 4 (Winter 1970), 110–16.

————. "Some Notes on the History of the Edward Taylor Manuscripts." *Yale University Library Gazette*, 39 (April 1965), 168–73.

Miller, Perry. *Errand into the Wilderness*. 1956. Reprint. New York: Harper & Row, 1964.

————. *Jonathan Edwards*. 1949. Reprint. Cleveland: World, 1959.

————. "Jonathan Edwards on the Sense of the Heart." *Harvard Theological Review*, 41 (April 1948), 122–45.

————. *The New England Mind*. 2 vols. Boston: Beacon Press, 1961.

————. "Solomon Stoddard, 1643–1729." *Harvard Theological Review*, 34 (October 1941), 277–320.

———— and Thomas H. Johnson, eds. *The Puritans: A Sourcebook of Their Writings*. 2 vols. 1938. Rev. ed. New York: Harper & Row, 1963.

Morison, Samuel E. *Builders of the Bay Colony*. Boston: Houghton-Mifflin, 1930.

————. *Harvard College in the Seventeenth Century*. 2 vols. Cambridge: Harvard University Press, 1936.

Murdock, Kenneth B. *Increase Mather, the Foremost American Puritan*. 1925. Reprint. New York: Russell & Russell, 1966.

————. "A Little Recreation of Poetry." *Literature and Theology in Colonial America*, pp. 152–72. 1949. Reprint. New York: Harper & Row, 1963.

Murphy, Francis. "Edward Taylor's Attitude toward Publication: A Question Concerning Authority." *American Literature*, 34 (November 1962), 393–94.

————, ed. *The Diary of Edward Taylor*. Springfield, Mass.: Connecticut Valley Historical Museum, 1964.

Neufield, Morris A. "A Meditation Upon the Glory of God." *Yale University Library Gazette*, 25 (January 1951), 110–11.

Norton, Arthur C. "Harvard Text Books and Reference Books of the Seventeenth Century." *Publications of the Colonial Society of Massachusetts*, 28 (April

1933), 361–438.

Nuttall, Geoffrey F. *The Holy Spirit in Puritan Faith and Experience.* Oxford: Blackwell, 1947.

O'Toole, Christopher. *The Philosophy of Creation in the Writings of St. Augustine.* Catholic University of America Philosophical Series, no. 81. Washington, D.C., 1944.

Patterson, Frank A., ed. *The Student's Milton.* New York: Appleton-Century-Crofts, 1961.

Peacham, Henry. *The Garden of Eloquence.* 1597. Facsimile reprint. Gainesville, Fla.: Scholars' Facsimile Reprints, 1954.

Pearce, Roy Harvey. "Edward Taylor: The Poet as Puritan." *New England Quarterly,* 23 (March 1950), 31–46. Reprint. *The Continuity of American Poetry,* pp. 42–54. Princeton: Princeton University Press, 1961.

Plato, *Great Dialogues.* Translated by W. H. D. Rouse. New York: New American Library, 1956.

"Poet in a Wilderness." *Times Literary Supplement,* 60 (February 3, 1961), 72. With letters to the editor by George L. Proctor (February 17, p. 105); Jack Lindsay (March 3, p. 137); and Donald Stanford (March 24, p. 185).

Prosser, Evan. "Edward Taylor's Poetry." *New England Quarterly,* 40 (September 1967), 375–98.

Reynolds, Edward. *A Treatise of the Passions and Faculties of the Soul of Man.* London, 1651.

Russell, Gene. "Dialectal and Phonetic Features of Edward Taylor's Rhymes: A Brief Study Based Upon a Computer Concordance of His Poems." *American Literature,* 43 (May 1971), 165–80.

Schaff, Philip, ed. *The Creeds of Christendom.* 3 vols. New York: Harper, 1882.

Sensabaugh, George F. *Milton in Early America.* Princeton: Princeton University Press, 1964.

Shepherd, Emma L. "Edward Taylor's Injunction Against Publication." *American Literature,* 33 (January 1962), 512–13.

————. "The Metaphysical Conceit in the Poetry of Edward Taylor (1644?–1729)." Ph.D. dissertation, University of North Carolina, 1960.

Simison, Barbara D. "Poems by Edward Taylor." *Yale University Library Gazette,* 28 (January-April 1954), 93–102, 161–70; 29 (July-October 1954), 25–34, 71–80.

Simpson, Allan. *Puritanism in Old and New England.* Chicago: University of Chicago Press, 1955.

Smyth, Egbert C. "Jonathan Edwards' Idealism." *American Journal of Theology* (October 1897), 950–64.

Sprunger, Keith L. "Technometria: A Prologue to Puritan Theology." *Journal of the History of Ideas,* 29 (January-March 1968), 115–22.

Stanford, Donald E. "The Earliest Poems of Edward Taylor." *American Litera-*

ture, 32 (May 1960), 136–51.

————. *Edward Taylor*. University of Minnesota Pamphlets on American Writers, no. 52. Minneapolis. 1965.

————. "Edward Taylor and the Lord's Supper." *American Literature*, 27 (May 1955), 172–78.

————. "Edward Taylor's Metrical History of Christianity." *American Literature*, 33 (November 1961), 279–95.

————. "Edward Taylor's 'Spiritual Relation.'" *American Literature*, 35 (January 1964), 467–75.

————. "Edward Taylor Versus the 'Young Cockerill' Benjamin Ruggles: A Hitherto Unpublished Episode from the Annals of Early New England Church History." *New England Quarterly*, 44 (September 1971), 459–68.

————. "The Giant Bones of Claverack, New York, 1705." *New York History*, 40 (January 1959), 47–61.

————. "Nineteen Unpublished Poems by Edward Taylor." *American Literature*, 29 (March 1957), 18–46.

————. Review of *Edward Taylor's Christographia*, edited by Norman S. Grabo. *American Literature*, 35 (May 1963), 242–43.

————. "*Sacramental Meditations* by Edward Taylor." *Yale University Library Gazette*, 31 (October 1956), 61–75.

————. "Two Notes on Edward Taylor." *Early American Literature*, 6 (Spring 1971), 89–90.

————, ed. "Edward Taylor's Metrical History of Christianity." Unpublished typescript, Yale University, 1962. Cleveland: Bell & Howell, Micro Photo Division, 1962.

————, ed. *The Poems of Edward Taylor*. New Haven: Yale University Press, 1960. Abridged edition. New Haven: Yale University Press, 1963. Originally "An Edition of the Complete Poetical Works of Edward Taylor." Ph.D. dissertation, Stanford University, 1953.

Taylor, Edward. "Diary." *Publications of the Massachusetts Historical Society*, 18 (April 1880), 5–18.

————. "Commonplace Book." MS, Massachusetts Historical Society, Boston, Massachusetts.

————. "Theological Notes." MS, Redwood Athenaeum, Newport, Rhode Island.

Thorpe, Peter. "Edward Taylor as Poet." *New England Quarterly*, 39 (September 1966), 356–72.

Tillyard, E. M. *The Elizabethan World Picture*. London: Chatto & Windus, 1943.

Tuve, Rosemond. *Elizabethan and Metaphysical Imagery*. Chicago: University of Chicago Press, 1947.

Underhill, Evelyn. *Mysticism*. London: Methuen, 1919.

Wadsworth, Benjamin. *The Well-Ordered Family*. Boston, 1712.

WORKS CITED

Waggoner, Hyatt H. "Edward Taylor." In *American Poets: From the Puritans to the Present*, pp. 16–24. Boston: Houghton-Mifflin, 1968.

Walzer, Michael. *The Revolution of the Saints: A Study in the Origins of Radical Politics*. Cambridge: Harvard University Press, 1965.

Warren, Austin. "Edward Taylor." In *Major Writers of America*, edited by Perry Miller. Vol. 1, pp. 51–82. New York: Harcourt, Brace & World, 1962.

————. *Rage for Order*. Chicago: University of Chicago Press, 1948.

Weber, Max. *The Protestant Ethic and the Spirit of Capitalism*. Translated by Talcott Parsons. New York: Scribner's, 1958.

Werge, Thomas. "The Tree of Life in Edward Taylor's Poetry: The Sources of a Puritan Image." *Early American Literature*, 3 (Winter 1969), 199–204.

Westfield "Church Record." MS, Edwin Smith Historical Museum, Westfield Athenaeum, Westfield, Massachusetts.

The Westfield Jubilee: A Report of the Celebration at Westfield, Mass. on the Two Hundredth Anniversary, pp. 152–59. Westfield: Clark & Story, 1870.

Willard, Samuel. *A Compleat Body of Divinity*. Boston, 1726.

Willey, Basil. *The Seventeenth Century Background*. London: Chatto & Windus, 1934.

Wolff, Cynthia G. "Literary Reflections of the Puritan Character." *Journal of the History of Ideas*, 29 (January-March 1968), 13–32.

Index

179

180